STUDENT BODIES

By Steve Ho
With a foreword by Rider
Cover art by Pepin Gelardi

THIS BOOK IS DEDICATED TO MY BROTHER AND MY BROTHERS.
ONE GAVE ME A SENSE OF HUMOR.
THE OTHERS SHOWED ME IT WAS NECESSARY.

RE-DEDICATED TO MARSHALL JAFFE
YOU LEFT US MUCH TOO SOON.

Acknowledgements

I thank the following people for the role they have played in this book, and in my life in general.

Rick Van Veen, Josh Abramson, Jakob Lodwick, and the rest of the CollegeHumor.com staff for all of their help in everything. Madeleine Morel and Tom Bunevich for their guidance. The Martin family for their advice and dessert. Cahill for the title. Pepin Gelardi for the cover. Kate Carcaterra for the photo. Rider for the foreword. The Math Fool for the, well, math. My family for their willingness to put up with me. My readers for giving me an audience (and more specifically Melissa and Lindsey for giving me an audience more than once a week, and Tori for having the balls to call me.) Points in Case, The Ape Sheet, My Professor Sucks, and Cara Engel for their support. The staff at the Spectator for being such rocking editors. Conrad Eberstein, John Beisler, Bill Tragos, Gary Kief, John Schuyler, Greg Lembrich, and Matt Matlack for their mentoring. New York Phi SigEp, for absolutely everything (except that trip to Syracuse). Susanna Fogel for her creativity. Professors Brady, Van Gelder, Julavitz, Jay, and McGlaughlin for their lessons. Joe Perello and UltraStar for taking a chance on me. Stephanie Geosits, Mark Mandrake, and Neil Schwartz for reminding me how much fun writing is. Shannon, Dov, Gordon, Joanna, Lee Ann, Fidyk, Amy, Haders, Nadine, Dana, Austin, Soze, Jelenko, Luis, Lowe, Amber, Memy, Marvin, Sarah, Rosy, DP, Viv, Fool, Mindy, Schenk, Smith, Whitney, Hilary, Ari, Nicole, Joel, Rick, Kate, B-Web, and Val for their unwavering friendship. And Yael - for challenging me to write what I want to write, all the while being one of the most kindhearted, caring and wonderful people I have ever met.

Printed in The United States of America

Library of Congress Cataloging-in-Publication Data

Hofstetter, Steve, 1979-
   Student body shots / by Steve Hofstetter.
        p. cm.
   ISBN 1-932133-60-7 (TP : alk. paper)
 1. College students—United States—Humor. 2.
College students—Humor. 3. College wit and humor.
I. Title.
   PN6231.C6H64 2003
   378.19'8—dc21
                                        200300
1706

The Writers' Collective

Published by The Writers' Collective
Cranston, Rhode Island

THE FOREWORD

By Rider Strong
Columbia University Class of ???

TV is about twenty years behind the times. I realized this when I was a freshman in college, while simultaneously playing a freshman on ABC's Boy Meets World. We would be doing a Very Special Episode about college dorm life, highlighting the value of your relationship with your best-friend-from-high-school-who-just-happens-to-also-be-your-college-roomate, and I would finish filming, go back to my dorm room to find my real roommate passed out on the floor, drunk. Obviously, he'd been having one of his own Very Special Episodes. Then there was the fact that on TV, our main characters were expressing their undying love to one another as vestal virgins, while everyone at my real school knew the one virgin in the incoming class. She lived down the hall…the freak.

I remember thinking that I could somehow have a "normal" college experience – an ideal blend of a Norman Rockwell painting and Animal House. Studying hard, making new friends, staying up for crazy nights, pizza, books, and spring breaks. All that was shattered the first day of orientation when everyone and their mother (literally) approached me on campus: "Hey, aren't you that guy from...?" "Hey look, it's that guy from...!" "You know who you look like, that guy from..." I was destined to be That Guy From. You'd be surprised how hard it is for people to remember a simple name like Boy Meets World: "Boys Meet World," "Boy Meets Girl," "Boy with the World," and that ever-present classic: "Boyses Meets the World."

But somewhere in my postmodern swirl of real college and its TV representation, I realized the fundamental lesson that every student learns at some point or another: there's no such thing as the "normal" college experience. By the time I graduate (someday, I pray) I will have been to three different schools, pretended to be a student in front of a camera for several roles, taken a million semesters off, taken countless half-semesters, and (this is my greatest accomplishment) never taken a math class. Thus, while Boy Meets World may have been far from normal, my own education hasn't been much closer, and really, has anybody's?

So, into the fractured subjectivity of college life, Steve Hofstetter has inserted this age-old wisdom: the only things that make college "normal" are the minute details we have in common, those little acts of stupidity ("I have to register *before* I show up to class?"), or naivete ("Who needs furniture?"), or college-level ingenuity ("If we break into the pool at night when it's closed, *then* we could go skinny-dipping!") that together we can look back upon, or forward to, shake our heads and gladly realize we're not alone. We're all in it together. And fortunately or unfortunately, someone like Steve is out there taking notes.

TABLE OF CONTENTS

"It's funny because it's true."

CHAPTER 1

WELCOME TO COLLEGE

One day, it's going to happen. You're going to look around and realize your parents are gone, your laundry is dirty, and you've gained, lost, and gained back fifteen pounds. You're in college. You'd call your parents and tell them, but they've stopped accepting the charges.

College is a non-stop whirlwind of excitement and IM, punctuated by hook-ups, drunken hook-ups, and failed attempts at hooking-up. There are plenty of aspects of college other than sex and alcohol, but those are the two that result in the most noise.

A problem arises when an author writes about their own college experience, focusing on aspects that do not relate to anyone outside his or her group of friends. That's like writing a paper on a movie your professor has never seen, but leaving out your interpretation of it as to not ruin the ending. Well, I'm here to spoil the ending for all of us: Indiana Jones made it out alive, Rocky won (again), and the boat sank--finally.

By the end of college, you will have had at least one hook-up that you regret. You will make and break a promise to never drink again, and you will waste anywhere between one and two hundred nights playing a number of bastardized versions of Tetris. You will invent a new recipe using Ramen or macaroni and cheese, familiarize yourself with the intricacies of Instant Messenger, learn how to gamble--or a combination of all three. You will study. You will forget everything you've learned. You will study again. You will keep forgetting. You will manage to squeak by anyway. And you will love every minute of it.

I may have just told you everything, but there's still a need to see the movie. The ending of college is not what's important – it's the journey that makes the film. So run to the lobby (bookstore) and make sure to get your popcorn (t-shirt with your school's name) and frosty beverage (halogen lamp). And get ready to watch one of the best documentaries that has ever been made—your own.

There's that Navy commercial that asks if someone made a movie of your life, would anyone go see it. Of course we would. Especially if Cuba Gooding Jr. isn't in it.

Welcome to college.

Choosing Schools

Half of prospective students want to go to the first school they visit. Everyone wants to go to the first school they drink at.

When my college counselor gave me the "how to get into a good school" seminar, I didn't trust a word she said. I fully intended to go to a good school and get a good job. All she knew how to do was go to a good school and become a college counselor.

If you know what you're doing with your life before you graduate high school, it's easy to pick a college. If you're one of those people who will change your major three times by junior year, it gets a little harder.

Choosing a college you visit is so arbitrary. Freshman year, a tour came through the day we had our spring concert. And those poor kids are thinking that Sonic Youth and Busta Rhymes play here every weekend.

I originally applied to Hunter College as my safety. Hunter is a good school, but it is basically made up of several class buildings in the middle of midtown Manhattan, interconnected by skyways that allow students to avoid the cabbies and bike messengers scurrying along below. That summer, I received a call from Hunter asking if I had made my decision yet. I apologized for not telling them my decision sooner, and explained that I would be attending Columbia University in the fall. The woman on the phone asked me if I had seen Hunter's campus. I thought about the dozens of times I had been to Hunter College before saying, "No, have you?"

There are three billion colleges that I've never heard of. And that's because so many schools are specialized now. "Oh, Jonathan Martin Smith University of South Carolina at Washington in Indiana? That's *the* school to go to if you want to major in Agricultural Marketing."

Do you remember how tough it was to pick a college? And aren't most of us happy with our choice? You know why? Because no matter what school we go away to, in no matter what state, with no matter what kind of people, as long as we don't live at home, everything seems to work out for the best.

Moving In

There's always one guy who is completely unpacked by noon of move in day. It takes me that long just to get the elevator.

The first time you move in to school, your entire family comes with you. They want to see the room - as if a ten-by-ten square with a bed, desk and closet could look unique. They're a help unpacking the twenty boxes and duffel bags you brought, but they stay way too long. All you want to do is meet people in your hall and get something to eat, but your mom has to arrange your pictures perfectly, you brother has to sit on your bed and complain that he wants to go home while not planning on getting up to go, and your dad has to tell you exactly which brand of light bulb you'll need to buy, as well as the history of the company that manufactures it. When you move back in sophomore year, you come by yourself and don't require help with anything. It's not because you learned how to pack more effectively or because you know exactly where your dorm is. It's because you remember how incredibly annoying it was to move in with your entire family the first time.

When you were in high school, the end of the summer was the worst thing in the world. In college, it's a godsend. You see all your friends, you no longer come back to your parents, and now when you drink on the weekends, there'll be someone there to safely drag you home.

Even if you bring nothing other than a simple sign that says "reserved," it is so very important that you get to your room before your roommate does. Arrival chronology dictates who gets which bed, the placement of all signs and posters, and which one of you has to buy the 300-foot Ethernet cord.

Guys – do not unpack right away. When you move in freshman year, the easiest way to meet girls is to go up and down the hall offering to put things on the top shelf.

By the time you graduate, you will have amassed a mini-fridge, stereo, TV, and VCR. Try to buy them before you move in, or you won't have anywhere to put your food after you listen to Pink Floyd while watching Dark Side of the Moon.

Orientation

My favorite orientation game is the one where you try to see how many people's names you can forget in one day.

Why do people volunteer to be orientation staff? This is the one week that all your friends will be in town with nothing to do but party. But hey, spending three days in meetings about how you can help orient people better, a day in 100-degree heat helping people move in while their parents complain to you about things completely out of your control, and then five more days tagging along with freshmen as they hook up with each other, looks great on a resume.

Orientation is a bad name for a week when everyone parties and has no classes. If I've learned anything about orientation week, it's that you're bound to wake up very disoriented.

Why do schools schedule any orientation programs before 10:00 AM? You can't even wake up for class by noon, why would you even think of getting up to hear about the detailed workings of the cafeteria? If it isn't going to be on the final, let me sleep through it.

My orientation advisor told me that by the end of the week, we'd be very *orientated*, and that gave me great confidence. Not because I had been nervous about not being "orientated," but because I figured if he could pass freshman composition, I'd be fine.

You can't always trust your orientation advisor to advise you properly. Remember – these are the same crazy people who are busy trying to help freshmen instead of trying to hook up with them.

If colleges really knew what students wanted, orientation would be different. You'd have a quiz on the campus map. You'd be issued your fake ID, and given a list of which bars will accept it. You'd receive a syllabus to every class (ranked in order of how much reading there is), and get a brochure about which foods to stay away from in the dining hall. You'd learn how to check your college email, get a tutorial on the first ten levels of Snood, and find out where all the Cliffs Notes are in the library. If all that doesn't prepare you for college, nothing will.

Meeting People

Starting a conversation would be easy if I could just go up to people and say, "Hi, I'm Steve." But you know why I don't? Because I know that one time someone will look at me and say, "so?"

Your first conversation with someone of the opposite sex is usually the best you'll have with them. "We stayed up til sunrise, just talking." True. But that's because you had twenty years to talk about. The problem now is that you've covered your whole life in one night, and now you're left with nothing for the rest of your friendship. "He just doesn't open up anymore." No, he's open - he's just got nothing left inside.

How many of you spent at least one of the first few nights of school with someone you met at an orientation program, sharing your lives until 5:00 AM? And, a semester later, how many of you spoke to that person more than once?

The worst is when a quiet guy works up the nerve to go up and talk to a girl, and as he gets there, she turns to talk to a friend of hers. Now, he's already standing there and his friends are watching, so he decides to wait. He stands there awkwardly. One sip of beer. Looks around to see if he knows anyone nearby,already knowing that he doesn't. Another sip of beer. Bobs his head to the music slightly, trying to look comfortable. Awkward pause. Another sip of beer. Another awkward pause. There is no sadder sight than a man who can't seem to cut into a conversation.

If you want someone new to like you, spend the first half hour of the conversation just asking questions. They'll talk about themselves, which everyone loves doing, and you won't have to risk saying something wrong. By the end, they will always say, "I feel like I know you so well."

I forget people's names right after I'm introduced to them. I'm concentrating so hard on remembering my own, I don't even hear theirs.

When you forget someone's name, the typical thing is to joke about how you were incredibly drunk when you met them. This works in college. This does *not* work in real life. "Oh, we met at that staff meeting last week? I'm sorry about that. I must have been totally wasted."

First Week of School

I've seen a lot of professors try to scare kids away on the first day of class by talking about all the work they'll be assigning. I wonder how those classes turned out.

At the beginning of every year, you swear you'll keep up with the readings and get all your assignments done in time. And every year, you do the first two assignments and then get lost behind a pile of backlogged work. You know why? Because the only difference between this year and last year is you being twelve months closer to drinking legally.

The best place to meet people is in class, on the first day of the semester. Almost any opening line works, but you usually can't fail with "Do you know anything about this professor?"

You know what the best part of coming back to school is? Pretending you weren't naive as a freshman. This year's freshmen haven't learned all the names of any of the buildings, can't distinguish any of the fraternities from each other, and think that they can get into a bar by swearing that they're twenty-one. But your class was different, right?

You see the greatest disparity in alcohol tolerance the first time people get back from the summer. Some of your friends haven't touched a beer since the night after their finals, and some have spent the entire summer on a first name basis with the local bartenders. Regardless of which camp you fall in, it's tough to walk home when half of you are puking and the other half are deciding which bar to go to next.

When a freshman girl hooks up with an older guy during the first week of school, she tells all her friends she met a smart, sophisticated, older man. If he were smart or sophisticated, she wouldn't be that far off.

Every floor has an uber-freshman. They get an ID from someone who looks nothing like them, drink three beers past their tolerance, and have only heard of one bar. They start every conversation with "where are you from?," hang that poster of John Belushi with his shirt that says "college," and play Dave Matthews mp3s on loop. Ignorance truly is bliss.

CHAPTER 2

THE DAILY GRIND

Alarm. Snooze. Alarm. Snooze. Roommate's alarm. Roommate's alarm. Throw something at roommate. Roommate's snooze. Alarm. Notice time. Shoot out of bed, late. Rinse, repeat.

Everyone at school has a different routine. Some include working out. Most include eating. But however you schedule your day, college is about routine. I think that's what Tim Robbins' Shawshank character said about prison, too. But the difference between us and inmates is that we have to pay tuition. And whether it's at a commuter school, a state school, or a grade-inflating private school, most of the daily grind is the same.

Our routines, which sometimes include classes and studying, are what define us. But it's the minutia that define them. Everyone sleeps at some point, though some less often than others. Everyone showers at some point, though again, some less often than others. We get dressed, eat, check our email, listen to music, check our email, use the phone, watch TV, check our email, and occasionally get real letters, after we check our email. We also recycle old routines, but no one usually notices because they're so busy with their own.

Freshman year, I set my alarm five minutes fast so that I could wake up in time for class. But I got used to it, so I tried seven minutes. By the time I did the math to figure out how much time I had, I was awake. When I got really good at subtracting seven, I moved my clock to the other side of the room. And when I learned to sleepwalk, I just started scheduling later classes. And thus, my new routine was born.

People outside college also have things like showers and food and email. But college puts a different spin on everything. People in the outside world don't need shower baskets or shower shoes. People in the outside world can't buy dinner with their IDs. And people in the outside world actually use the phone. Sometimes.

When our parents went to school, much of the daily grind was the same. The only real difference is the technology, and beyond that, this is the same stuff that's been going on for decades and decades. The curriculum at my school hasn't changed in 200 years, why should dorm life be any different? This is the daily grind.

Sleep

It's a glorious feeling to be walking home at 6:00 AM and see everyone's parents up at the crack of dawn, on their way to work. And even better to see that guy on the crew team do it.

Nothing good ever happens to anyone while they sleep. Most of the good stuff in college happens about ten or fifteen minutes beforehand.

Some people use their lack of sleep as an excuse for being a moron. They crack some dumb joke, and then try to get out of it by saying "Oh man, I must be really tired." But if you woke up a dumbass, odds are its because you went to sleep a dumbass. What do you think happens if you sleep for twenty-seven hours? You wake up and win a nobel prize? No, you wake up a very well rested dumbass.

Before college, you don't need sleep. You went to bed at 12:00 and woke up at 6:00 and were fine with it. Now you go to sleep at 2:00 and wake up at 10:00 and you've never been more tired.

When someone calls me before 11:00 on a weekend, if someone isn't already dead, they're going to be.

When you're not tired, you can never really remember how tired you were, because being tired passes. But when you are tired, you can never remember anything.

Staying awake all night while you're having fun is a smart idea. Face it: you can always sleep later. But staying awake just to be awake isn't so smart. You might not be able to watch infomercials and read everyone's away messages another time, but is that really such a bad thing?

My mom used to wake me up by calling me too early in the morning. It took me freshman year to explain that Friday is part of the weekend.

When vacation comes, all you want to do is sleep. And then you wind up staying up until dawn doing nothing in particular, just because you can. You do this for weeks, until you have to go back to class. Which is when you say, "man I could use some sleep."

Showers

Seeing some people in a towel is a good thing. But for the rest of you, have some respect for your hall-mates and change in the bathroom. Nothing says good morning like a fat wet guy in a mini-towel.

I got fed up with everyone using my shampoo when I left it in the bathroom, so I scrawled my name all over the bottle. From then on, at least they knew who it was that they didn't care about pissing off.

The second most important thing you can buy for college is a good set of shower shoes. The most important thing you can buy is a can of industrial-strength disinfectant for the day after you were too drunk to care about shower shoes.

I guess I can understand sex in the public shower if it's a one-person bathroom. But in one of those multi-person bathrooms? Maybe I'm weird, but I don't see the sounds of people relieving themselves as all that conducive to getting it on.

Some people can get away with showering less than once a day. No one can get away with showering less than once a month.

I'm surprised that college girls aren't all incredibly strong. With the amount of crap they carry back and forth from the shower every day, they should be able to kick the ass of any guy that limits themselves to a bottle of shampoo and a towel.

How much could shower stalls actually cost? There's enough money to throw an "RA Pizza Party!" every week, but guys still have to shower with everyone on their hall like they were at the Y.

Water pressure is not the key to life. But it is certainly the key to getting to class on time.

You can tell a lot about someone by what they keep in their shower basket. Four different shampoos means they're obsessed with their appearance. Neat labels mean they're anal. And a tube of foot fungus means they probably forgot to buy shower shoes.

Fashion

Are you in a class with that one really unique guy who tries to find all the vintage clothes he can because it makes him stand out from the rest of the crowd? I'm in a class with thirty-eight of them.

Most people can't wear short sleeve button paisley shirts. But most people don't have British accents.

What impresses me most about cold weather is that no matter how bad it gets, some girls will still not wear coats to bars. If guys cared as much about looking good rather than being warm, the wool-hat-with-the-little-beanie-on-top industry would take a serious hit.

I saw a huge woman wearing a shirt that said "USA." I think she did a pretty good impression.

People couldn't wear ugly clothes if clothing companies stopped making them. Although I'm pretty sure this one girl in my history class would figure out how.

Why don't girls who want play just go up to a guy and invite him back to their room? Because that would be unladylike. Yeah, and wearing that tube top and leather pants outfit is perfectly dignified.

Girls, you know what will make you stand out at a bar? Wear black pants, a solid pastel-colored low-cut top, boots, and big hoop earrings. But here's a real tip - we do not care what you are wearing, as long as we can convince ourselves you won't be wearing it for much longer.

Free clothes from school events are cool for now, but after you graduate, they get a little useless. I'm going to be twenty-five and have two dozen t-shirts that say "Columbia Community Outreach" and "CU Safer Sex Week". Won't those be a hit around the office.

I always prefer comfort over style. I wear a coat to bars when it's cold out, I take layers off in class when it's warm out, and I don't think that either one hurts my chances to attract girls. If my teeth were chattering or my pits were stained - now *that* would hurt my chances.

Television

There should be a channel devoted to television commercials. They'd show half-hour blocks of all the best Coke commercials, Budweiser ads, and Wendy's spots. And they could have breaks where they show three-minute clips of sit-coms so you can go to the bathroom without missing anything.

There's one CD compilation that advertises "today's hottest dance music", and they lead with C&C Music factory. I bought it right away, and then I put on my leg warmers and snap bracelets and roller-skated to the premier of "Rambo."

It's okay for a college to make a TV commercial. But at least use students that aren't frightening. Do you remember that old commercial for Drake Institute, with everyone saying, "Hey Drake, give me a break"? My favorite was the guy who said, "Ha Dwaake, ge ma a baaake." That year, there was a thirty percent increase in applications among students who sounded like they were melting.

The E! True Hollywood story says that they tell the story you never heard. Dana Plato? Mariel Hemmingway? Herve Villachez? Sure I've never heard those stories. I wasn't listening.

Have you ever seen "Street Smarts"? That's the show where a host walks around malls and parks to prove that society is crumbling.

My impression of the Psychic Friends Network: "I'm looking at the taro cards and they tell me that your life sucks. That'll be $2.95." Of course your life sucks - you're calling the damn Psychic Friends Network. How hard would it be to guess this guy's future? "The cards are telling me that you live in a trailer, work at Arby's, and one of your relatives just died - otherwise you wouldn't have enough disposable income to call me."

Have you ever seen those rascal commercials? It's that motorized chair, and their big thing is that they give away a free one every once in a while. Everyone says "I got my free rascal" in this really weird way. Apparently, it comes with a complimentary lobotomy.

Food

Only in a college town can you get a hot dog and cheese fries at 3:00 AM. And only in a college town will you have to spend ten minutes on a line while you wait for it.

College students will put their dishes in the sink, but they'll never go to the trouble to put them in a dishwasher right next to it. Why? The same reason that all of our laundry is on the floor instead of in the closet, and we throw up in the hallway instead of the bathroom. When you're that drunk, doors can be very tricky.

My advice is to try to get a dorm with a kitchen. That way you have a place to keep the forks you use to eat all the take-out Chinese food you get every night instead of cooking.

There's a half-Chinese, half-Spanish restaurant near me. I don't know what they serve, but I'm pretty sure it has rice.

My first time in Starbucks, I asked for a small hot chocolate. The guy behind the counter said, "oh, you mean a tall." I said, "no, a small." He said, "tall is our smallest size." I said, "your company does not understand basic weights and measures." He said, "Next."

I think the worst thing about Starbucks is that there are people who think that there's nothing wrong with Starbucks. Then again, these are the same people who can order a Mocha Frappaccino with a straight face.

Meriam-Websters defines "edible" as "fit to be eaten." College students define it as "there."

If you think coffee bars are annoying, a tea bar opened a block off my campus. How pretentious is that? I want to just order "tea" and see what happens. "What's that? Be specific? Sure. I'd like a small tea."

My senior year, I wanted to make a sandwich, but I only had one piece of bread left. So instead of folding it in half, I put the bread between two slices of cheese. And I thought, "man, I'm going to miss college."

Money

Why can I spend forty bucks in a bar in one night, but refrain from ordering extra cheese because I don't want to blow the fifty cents?

Why do bums ask college students for money? "Excuse me, I know that you've been wearing the same socks for eight days in a row to avoid the cost of laundry, never have a steady girlfriend because picking up a girl at a bar and going back to your room is cheaper than a movie, and rely on your parents for a ride home after finals cause the train costs too much, but can you spare a dollar?"

When you are in college, a roll of quarters is like pure gold. You need them for laundry, vending machines, and payphones. I bet you could make a pretty good living walking up and down dorm hallways selling three quarters for a dollar.

There's always one guy on every floor who panhandles. He goes from room to room, saying "dude, you got a quarter I could borrow for laundry?" By the end of the day, he's made thirty bucks and sitting there in the lounge eating a whole pizza.

Sophomore year, you can tell who is a businessman by who is not on meal plan anymore. They just get the thirteen bucks in cash from their parents, eat a slice of pizza, pocket the difference, and buy and sell chumps who are still on the meal plan.

The only kind of money college students ever have is a twenty dollar bill. Since ATMs only give out twenties, you end up going to dinner with five people and no one has change. One guy ends up covering it, and everyone says they'll pay him back as soon as they get change. Which never happens.

Some people put things on their parents' credit card. If I could do that, my parents would have been jailed three times by sophomore year.

When you're in college, you learn to eat on ten bucks a week, and it's not because you're paying $30,000 a year. It's because you're paying eight dollars a pitcher.

E-mail

It'd be great if you got other things with the same excitement that AOL gives you when you get mail. Like STD results. "Welcome! You've got crabs!"

You can tell what kind of people your friends are by what they forward you. If your friend sends you a good joke, they are funny. If they send you a virus warning or a promise of money from Bill Gates, they are gullible. And if they send you constant poems about what friendship means, tweety birds drawn with asterisks, and pleas from the cancer foundation, I give them ten years before they'll be handing out pamphlets in an airport.

The dumbest commercial I've ever seen is for AOL. The guy says, "My friend said, 'Try AOL.' I said, 'Why, I already have a computer.'" Yeah, genius, that's the point. Is the same guy that needs directions on toothpaste and shampoo? "Rinse *and* repeat? You sure?"

The dumbest forwards I have seen are the pleas for kids with cancer. Not to be insensitive, but even if tracking email were *remotely* possible, why would the cancer society donate three cents for every forward? Wouldn't they be the ones collecting donations?

I understand getting a virus off a disk. But I have no sympathy for people who get viruses via e-mail. A few years ago, the "I love you" virus spread across the world and it was the saddest thing I had heard in a long time. Talk about preying on people's insecurities. "Hey Joe, come in here quick! Not only did my boss from my internship last summer send me an e-mail, but he loves me! And he apparently wants me to download this file..."

Do you know the one guy who checks his email only once a week because he says he doesn't want to be a slave to technology? And what's more important, do you have his cell phone number?

It's fun to sign your roommate up for junk mail. It's really fun to sign him up to the same lists once a month, and then watch as he gets into email fights about whether or not he already unsubscribed.

Computers

When your computer breaks, and it will, most college tech support people can't help you. But man, are they good at Counter Strike.

There will always be jobs for people good with computers. Because there will always be files deleted by people who aren't.

I know some people whose parents pay for their entire tuition, their cars, and their meal plan, but won't buy them a computer. I'm not saying parents need to buy their kids everything they want. I'm just saying that if you're buying your kid a round of golf, you might want to make sure he has a set of clubs.

On-line gambling is dangerous because credit cards let you go into debt too quickly. So I have a friend who checks his e-mail once a day and lets people bet the over/under on how many messages he got.

Computers make mailing real letters worth so much more. Writing someone an actual letter is like asking a college girl out to dinner. Sure, it's easy and an every day thing that your parents did all the time. But because so few other people think of it, you're a hero.

I laugh when I see a news story about how knowledge of an email or a web page spread around the world in just a few days. Of course it did – that's how this stuff works. It takes just seconds to tell your whole address book that all your base are belong to us, ninjas are totally sweet, and you wanna go 'weeeeeeee' but you ain't got drugs yet. Telling your friends about a cool web page is like being able to say "quick, turn on channel seven" to thirty people at once. And to have channel seven be the same three days later.

No one ever takes notes on laptops during class. They write their papers for other classes, but no one ever takes notes.

Do you remember having a 2400 speed modem? Do you remember your first 100 megabyte hard drive? Do you remember the time you spent fondly reminiscing with your friends about how small and slow your computers used to be? God, I hope not.

Phones

How do people sleep through their phone ringing fifty times? If the phone ringing for five minutes straight doesn't wake you, why the hell do you own an alarm clock?

I had a class once where this one girl got calls on her cell phone every time. I'm not sure which was harder to believe - that she was so dumb that she never once thought to shut her phone off, or that she could carry on a conversation well enough to make someone want to call her between the hours of 2:40 and 3:55 every Tuesday and Thursday.

Everyone knows that when they go home for the summer, they try dialing 9 to get an outside line. But the worst are the people like me who go to schools with seven-digit access codes. There's got to be some old woman out there that has my access code as her phone number, wondering who the hell keeps calling her at 2:00 AM trying to get some pizza.

Ever wonder how the woman on your voicemail got her job? Did she bring in her answering machine as her demo tape? "I've mostly done local stuff, but I was really thinking of branching out, you know, getting more exposure. Where do I see myself in five years? 'Hello. The current time is 3:00 PM.' I know that's reaching, but a gal can dream, can't she?"

I hate broadcast phone messages. At my school, they're always about string quartets or classes I'm ineligible to take. We have parties once a month where seniors get free beer. And I've never once been able to wake up to a voice mail about it.

Why is it that the technology for call-waiting eludes most major universities? "Sure, we have call waiting here. Just press 8, followed by the pound key, and your seven digit access code. Then, hang up for no less than three and no more than four seconds, and enter your current weight, followed by your sixth grade locker combination. To return to the first call, simply repeat those steps, in descending alphabetical order." When anyone looks at colleges, they should look for academics, sports, a social scene, and a decent phone system.

Mail

Some kids get packages from their parents every week. Other kids already have plenty of AA batteries, tube socks, and crushed up cookies from their grandmothers.

Are college mailrooms the minor leagues of the post office? "I want you to know this is the hardest part of a manager's job. Jim, you're not disgruntled enough. If you snapped, you'd kill one, maybe two people at the most. We're going to have to send you down for rehab."

How many of you have parents that send you newspaper clippings from your local paper? Cause when you go to USC, you can't wait to hear all about the beauty pageant in Gary, Indiana.

The problem with sending promotional mail to colleges is that students only have their addresses for one year. And every time a new student gets on a mailing list, their junk mail gets added to the queue. So every month, some poor kid gets seventeen catalogues from Radio Shack.

Sometimes the post office screws up and mangles a letter. But the best is when they send you one of those "sorry we mangled your letter" envelopes complete with the scraps of what's left. I've gotten two so far—one was the corner of a postcard, and the other had tire tracks on it.

There was a big scandal at Columbia last year when we found out that some of the students' mail was being thrown out. Somehow, we all still got our phone bills.

It's so much fun to get packages at school because the potential for what's inside is virtually limitless. And that fun is almost enough to make it worthwhile to wait on line for an hour while the guy behind the package desk finds everyone's box but yours.

I had a friend who would sign up on mailing lists just so he'd get mail, and then he'd throw it out the second he saw it was junk. Why even get your hopes up? Getting junk mail is like having an A on your paper, with "Just kidding, you got a C" scribbled beneath it.

Instant Messenger

People lose all inhibition over IM. You can confess your love, tell someone off, or make crude sexual jokes that would otherwise be inappropriate. It's like being drunk but without the beer. Or the play.

I feel bad for the people who spend so much time working on their profile that it becomes a pathetic last-ditch effort at a free personal ad. "Single white male gets turned on by long walks on the beach, Harry Belafonte, and typing 'lol.'"

Some people don't sign on much because they're afraid of being bombarded. I don't know which is harder to believe - that someone hasn't grasped the concept of saying "can I talk to you later?" or that a bombardment worth of people would want to talk to anyone that slow.

Almost everyone, at some point or another, quotes a song in their away message, but changes the lyrics slightly to apply to what they're doing. Oh, I get it - it's been a hard day's night, but instead of just working like a dog, you're working like a dog - in the library! How galactically clever!

A random IM is okay, but only if you begin the conversation. One day I'm going to call people and hang up right after I say hello, shake hands and walk away, and write letters that only say "Dear Jim."

I wish you could pause over the phone like you can on IM. All the time, I'd start a phone conversation with someone, talk to them for five minutes, and then just put the phone down and walk away. An hour later I'd come back and say "Sorry - my roommate came in. Gotta run to class!" and then hang up before they could say anything.

People can be witty over IM. People can be charming over IM. People can not be hot over IM. "I can tell by your clever use of italics and your intermittent 'lol'ing that you have a nice ass." Hey buddy - those yellow happy faces may be cute, but they're not quite accurate.

Imagine if Shakespeare wrote with the same casualness that people use over IM. "2b or not 2b," "Where RU, romeo," and "U 2, brute?" just don't seem to carry the same weight as the originals.

It's awesome that you can check your e-mail on your cell phone now. But using IM? Sure, it's great to be able to send a quick message to your friend. Of course, it'd be easier if you had some sort of phone handy...

Bootie-calling is pretty skeezy. But it has nothing on the booty-IM. At least with calling, you think of everyone you know and you call the person who is most likely to respond. With IMing, you choose between the two people on your buddy list who are still awake.

"Lol" means "laugh out loud" and "rofl" means "rolling on the floor laughing," but people constantly use them in the wrong place. "No, I'm laughing, I swear. In fact, I am actually rolling on my floor, but I can miraculously still type." If you want to stop people from doing this, start using "lol" in person. Nothing kills a joke faster than turning to whoever told it and emphatically saying, "That's hysterical! Lol!"

Being drunk is great sometimes because you can say whatever you want and get away with it. But unlike the phone or in person conversations, drunk IM could be really easy to fake. All you need is a program that capitalizes stuff, takes out half of your vowels, and switches every fifth letter to the key next to it.

You can get people's screen names using their e-mail address, but most people don't know that and get freaked if you look them up that way. I bet it was like that when phone books first came out. "You mean there's a huge book with everyone's phone number in it? And all you need to know is their name! My god, technology is incredible! God bless the 1990s!"

I understand that some people use ICQ in addition to Instant Messenger. But I don't get the people who use it instead. It may be better quality, but I use what's universal. When someone asks me my ICQ number, that's like buying a Beta VCR and trying to rent the Matrix.

Some situations call for being more casual than usual, and IM is definitely one of them. But abbreviations like "4get" and "UR" are a bit too casual for any situation. Put it this way - if the rest of the world is wearing pants, it's not the best idea to sit around in your boxers.

Music

When I meet a guy, I want to ask, "what kind of guitar do you play?"

Want a fun experiment? Walk into a room full of college girls and play 80s music - especially Madonna, Guns 'N' Roses, or Bon Jovi - and they will all instinctively jump up and down for a few seconds, then sing into their hand like it's a microphone while they lean about thirty degrees toward each other in a circle.

A capella groups are like college basketball teams. Some can run successful programs for decades at a time. But most lose their stars every few years and have to rebuild, regardless of what their name used to mean. Also, the people involved in the bad ones never score.

I can understand why bands form. But I can't understand why cover bands form. Sure, Billy Joel has millions of fans, but you can play Piano Man better. Especially on guitar.

You know MP3s have taken hold when everyone has burnt copies of all the CDs from their music class.

I think live music is usually better than listening to a CD. But I will never understand why people like recorded live music better than something produced in a studio. "Hey, he's saying something to the live audience that we can't really hear. Oh, I love when he does stuff like that! Maybe later, he'll miss a few notes, and the mic will pick up some feedback!"

I love those compilation CDs they sell on TV. When it's one I want to buy, I get the song list off their website, download all the tracks, burn the CD myself, and spend the $19.95 on pizza.

Why do people who get rejected from one a cappella group start their own? If you get cut from the basketball team, do you start another?

I am a music idiot. I like popular music with a good beat and good lyrics, and I don't care how studio produced it is, how few chords it uses, or how little talent it took to play. That's the only way I can play it on my guitar anyway.

Your Fat Friend
A Student Body Shots Song

The chords here are pretty simple - Gs, Cs, and Ds. But if your cover band can come up with a better progression or a good version of this one, record the mp3 and send it to collegehumor@yahoo.com. Look at that - this book is interactive.

Note: This song is not at all meant to be an afront to fat people. This song is meant to be an afront to fat people with bad personalities. If you are a fat person with a fun personality, like Santa Claus or Al Roker, I wish you nothing but the best.

I agreed to meet you out today, the corner bar was fine
I figured I would get you drunk and then you'd be all mine
We sat and drank and talked and drank
And drank and drank and then
Out of the corner of my eye I noticed...
Your fat friend

All hands on deck, look out below - there walks the mangy cuss!
Avast ye mates, and thar she blows, she's coming right for us
I grab your hand and walk away
So that we won't be sighted
But with five words, you ruin my night: "Hey Steve...
She was invited"

"You two would get along just fine," you say. "She's really sweet.
"I'm sure she is," I say right back. But who did she just eat?
And now my quest to score tonight
Has reached a bitter end
And I know that its all because I'm here...
With your fat friend

I'm all for personality, I think brains are a goal
But not when you are terrified that she could eat you whole

Ladies, I'll be honest here
So you don't misconstrue
When guys say you should bring a friend, we mean...
Who looks like you.

You say "Look past the pounds of flesh to realize what's inside."
I tried to look beyond her but my vision's not that wide
Lets cut the bull and set it straight
There's no need to pretend
That I can take another minute here...
with your fat friend

I could not help but speculate, "My god, what could be worse?"
Her handkerchief could be my towel, I'd fit inside her purse
But as I try to get away
And fend off the attack
You stand up and you walk away and say...
"I'll be right back."

I sit and listen to her drone about some boring crap
I can't help but think I've fallen into some god-awful trap.
Let me put this in a way
That she can comprehend
I do not like green eggs and ham and I...
hate your fat friend.

Well I like you, you know I do, but I can not tolerate
That I sit here and wait for you and she just sits with weight.
Her hips are the corruption
Of a sick American dream
And I can't think of a reason that I'd take...
one for the team.

I say this with all honesty, and with my complete candor
Guys, chin up and have respect for yourselves and what you stand for
I don't mean to discourage you
And I don't mean to offend
She doesn't want to date you if she leaves you there...
with her fat friend.

CHAPTER 3

PIECES OF THE PUZZLE

Have you ever put a puzzle together, and towards the end, you've got a few pieces left that look the same? So you try them all in different combinations with each other until one of them sort of fits, and you just jam it in so that you can finish, but end up breaking the damn thing instead. I call that "sophomore year."

There are probably as many metaphors for college as there are kids on your hall who like Dave Matthews, but one of my favorites is the puzzle. See, in a puzzle, the ends are the easiest part to figure out. But the middle is kind of hazy. Kind of like a Saturday.

The puzzle includes all things college, but I've picked out a few that strike me as the most common. Facebooks, language, sports, shopping, gambling, laundry, weather, travel, being sick, and glasses have effects that can be found on every hallway. Especially in that one room where the well-dressed foreign athlete with a cold is buying new glasses because he wants to read the facebook but he lost his old glasses in a poker game. Or something.

And the puzzle metaphor pretty much holds true throughout college. There are some pieces that are easier to see than others, because they are part of a clear section of the larger whole. But others just have to be plugged in to what's already there until you see something recognizable. And when you're finally done putting it all together, and the whole thing is complete, you tell your parents and you take a picture.

There are other metaphors, too. Like a buffet, where you can take as much or as little as you'd like, but you have to eat what course load you take. Or the quilt, where everything is interwoven, and it's more aesthetic than it is useful. Or college being one of those cheese and cracker gift baskets, where everything tastes great, but it's in too small a serving to really enjoy. But I still prefer the puzzle idea. Maybe because I'm better at puzzles than I am at college, and the idea that this thing actually has a correct solution is a nice one.

And though I can't offer you that solution, I can at least describe what the pieces look like. The real world is probably a puzzle, too, but I bet it's one of those fancy 3-D things that you just leave in the box until your nerdy friend comes over and solves it for you.

Facebooks

There is no interests section in the facebook. You know why? No one wants to flip through a book to find out which girls play chess.

Every campus has one fraternity that has a facebook party - where they look up all the hot girls and invite them over. And even sadder than the guys who are patting themselves on the back for coming up with the idea are the girls who show up. What these girls don't realize is that the words "freshmen" and "fresh meat" are spelled very similarly.

There was one girl in my facebook whose head was obviously cut out of another picture and put in front of a plain background. What horrible thing could she have possibly been standing in front of that she took all that trouble for a half-inch headshot?

No one knows what a facebook is until they get to school. So when your school asks you for a photo over the summer, you figure it's probably for their records. Then for the next four years, you're the guy who slept on his hair funny.

If schools are going to put out facebooks, they may as well include measurements.

The problem with the facebook is that one day, it will ruin you. You'll meet a really hot girl in a bar, and you'll swear you remember her from somewhere. You exhaust all your classes, mutual friends, and extra-curriculars, until you finally realize that she's page twenty-three, fourth column down, third picture from the left, whose photo you spent orientation week staring at and showing to all your friends. And how do you start a conversation with that?

Wouldn't it be great if all schools put their facebooks on hotornot.com? Then graduating with a 4.0 would not be quite as respectable as it used to be.

If you think that people in the facebook will look hotter in real life, you're wrong. You can subtract ten pounds for what the camera added, but you'll have to add fifteen for what happens during freshman year.

Language

When I got to college, I learned that everyone here speaks differently. We all use words like "sketchy" and "tool" that no one ever uses back home. That's why I don't go home any more. Because when I do, no one will understand me.

Every school has it's own terminology, and we all forget that it's different at every campus. It took my friend from Dartmouth five minutes to explain to me that "blitzing" meant checking his e-mail. We all call our mailrooms, libraries, and dining halls by their last names; at Columbia, it's Lerner, Butler, and Jay. Hey, no one outside of your campus knows what the hell you're talking about. Shut up and call them "mailrooms," "libraries," and "dining halls."

Most people learn the words they use from listening to other people speak. This is why I'm puzzled that some professors are so out of it when it comes to slang. The saddest thing is to see the professors that are out of touch convince themselves that they can be "hep," "cool," and even "down with that." I actually had a teacher tell me once that "there are some things with which one should not get jiggy." Ouch.

When you hang out a lot with one person or a close knit group of friends, you forget that some people don't understand your inside jokes. This is why I've never had two girlfriends - I'd constantly be making references to things that only one of them understands.

In any group of friends, there's always the phrase guy. The one guy who says all these cool phrases that everyone copies for a semester, until he says a new cool phrase that they can copy. In a big group of friends, there are two or three of these guys. In a fraternity, they're called "the executive board."

I was riding in a cab and I heard boxing announcer Michael Buffer as the celebrity welcome voice. His line was "Let's get ready to rumble - for safety!" Sweet - then we can have a knife fight for world peace.

There needs to be a special dictionary for students. Since the 1980s, how often is the word "pong" really used outside of college?

Sports

Folks, lets be honest. You are a group of ten guys from your freshman dorm. You will not beat the football team at any intramural sport. Especially football.

Some football teams have drinking problems. Some drinking teams have football problems.

I was afraid I'd get my ass kicked for making fun of college sports. But those who would have kicked my ass can't read this in the first place.

Athletes wear clothes with their team name. But I think if you're wearing your team name, you should be willing to wear your record, too. Nothing will get you to change faster than everyone seeing "3-7" on your jacket.

I can understand the athletes at schools like Duke and Ohio State thinking they're all that. But the second saddest thing in the entire world is a D3 football player on a losing team who has a big ego anyway. The saddest thing is the girl that will hook up with him based on it.

If the kicker is considered the bitch of a pro team, and college teams are below pro teams, and my school's football team is widely known as one of the worst college teams in the country, what does that make our kicker? And what does that make our second string kicker? It'd be like working at a prison. In Siberia. As the janitor. On weekends.

I was told that athletes at Duke and Stanford have it tougher than those at other sports schools like Maryland or USC because of the rigorous academics. Yeah, the seven-foot kid who can't speak English but manages to be a communications major has it real tough.

We have intramural quiz bowl at my school. So we play football, basketball, softball, soccer, and jeopardy.

Most guys, at one point or another, want to play an intramural sport with their friends. Just like most guys, at one point or another, want to open a bar with their friends. Except no one buys the bar. But one guy will always show up with a ball and wonder where his friends went.

Shopping

When I buy clothes, I keep them. You know why girls go shopping all the time? Because they've run out of stuff to lend other girls.

Some people suggest that you should make friends with the person on your floor with a car. I think your time is better spent pursuing that one kid who always says, "that's okay, it's my parents credit card."

Hey guys, want to see something great? Tell your female friends that you're going clothes shopping and watch every one of them beg to come with you. For a girl, guys are the ultimate male dress up dolls. Except a girl never tried to convince Ken to buy a $1200 suit.

There are three things that can be very dangerous to do while drunk. Operating heavy machinery, calling your ex, and online shopping. All three could cost you a few body parts.

I've gotten so used to online shopping that I have a hard time buying anything at a store. "You mean I can actually own this today? What do you mean, there's no shipping and handling?"

Why don't department stores have a special section for kids going away to college? Do they understand how much money they could make just selling shower baskets, Yaffa blocks, and dry erase boards?

No one buys stuff with their college's name on it after the first week of school, because you eventually realize that you can't wear it anywhere. If I wear Columbia stuff around campus, people look at me like, "yeah, me too. So what?" If I wear it at home, all my mom's friends want to talk to me for an hour about how I like school. Instead, I always try to wear my Columbia shirts to sleep. Nothing helps a hangover like a stark reminder of my Ivy League education.

At the end of my senior year, all of the seniors got together and held a giant yard sale where we could get rid of all of the extra crap that we weren't going to bring to our new apartments. And you know who bought it? A bunch of professors who had kids that were about to go to college, and seemingly needed lots of extra crap to bring with them.

Gambling

Maybe winning at a slot machine is such a great feeling because you don't do it enough to get used to it.

I figured out the perfect system for winning at roulette. Come with me, and bet on everything I don't bet on.

Don't ever think that you've figured out a fool-proof system for winning at any game in a casino. These guys do this for a living. If there were a way to beat the odds, they'd change the odds. You know why they call them odds? Because if you go in thinking that you're actually the first guy to ever come up with betting on black five times in a row, well, that's pretty odd.

I wonder if people who play slots get excited when they vote. "Cherry! Cherry! Oh, Libretarian."

You do not have a gambling problem when you blow $1,000 on the Final Four. You have a gambling problem when you blow $1,000 on women's high school wrestling.

With both poker and asshole, you should only gamble if you can afford to lose. You could be the best player in the world, but unless you have a big stomach, you might end up face down in your own vomit. And you might lose at asshole, too.

College kids can't gamble away all of our money. We don't have any.

Poker and darts are very important skills to learn while still in college. How else are we going to train for careers in finance and city planning?

When I play poker with someone for the first time, I buy a case of beer. Sure, I spent a few bucks, but I'll win it back from the drunk guy that's betting twenty bucks on a pair of twos.

I don't like football pools that take the knowledge of the game out of the equation. I know a lot about sports. I know very little about successfully choosing things out of a hat.

Laundry

How many times have you gone to the laundry room without enough change to do a load? As many times as you've spent the next five minutes looking under the folding tables, behind each machine, and through all of your pants pockets for the elusive extra quarter.

People are hypocrites about laundry. One day, your friend will complain about the guy who left his laundry in the washer for fifteen minutes, until your friend finally moved the clothes to a table and put his own wash in. Two weeks later, your same friend will complain about the gall someone had to move their stuff out of a washer when they were only fifteen minutes late to retrieve it.

Do not buy laundry detergent in bulk. Sure, it seems cheaper, but it's just big enough to convince you to lend it to everyone on your hall until you have to buy a new one.

You know that one room in every dorm that is kept locked at all times? It's full of half pairs of socks, collected from your laundry by the desk attendant . Eventually, enough students come through a dorm that pairs begin to form, and are sold on the street at a 50% markup. How do you think he affords that stereo he's always listening to?

Are you one of the poor saps who refuses to invest $3.95 in a laundry basket? You try to carry two loads of clothes in your arms, drop two shirts and three pairs of boxers on the way to your room, and have to position the stack on one knee and one hand, pressed against the wall, while struggling to open your door with the hand that has to catch all the socks that are hitting the floor. And you do this every two weeks.

Guys joke about having 365 pairs of boxers so they can do laundry once a year. But imagine how horrible it would be to do that load.

You know that day where you finally get to the clothes you try to never wear? You walk to class in jeans with a rip in the left leg and a pizza stain on the right, a paint-covered t-shirt from the community service project you were roped into freshman year, and a pair of socks missing half the heel and all the toes. And you do your laundry three days later.

Weather

Every year, I have to buy a new scarf. I'm not sure why I can never keep a scarf in the same place for the nine months I don't use it, but I guess it's impossible. Once, I tried keeping my scarf in the arm of my winter coat. That year, I had to buy a new coat.

Spring is year-round in some places. But in the Northeast, it snows until late March. My friend once made a snow sculpture of a tropical drink with a little umbrella in it. I hope God appreciated the irony.

The thing that I dread most about good weather is "ugly warm day". The first day it's warm enough for shorts and tight shirts, everyone wears them, regardless of how disgustingly ugly they are. Suddenly, you realize that those puffy North Face coats aren't such a bad thing.

Kids who grew up with snow always make fun of the kid from California who thinks three inches is a blizzard. The same thing happens in California when a New Yorker dives for cover the first time they feel the ground shake. "Oh come on! It couldn't be more than a 3.2. They're not even closing the roads. Get out from under the desk. Wussy."

After a long hot summer, the weather hits fifty degrees and you rummage through your closet to find your coat, scarf, gloves, and wool hat. But after just one week of winter, your view changes. "It's fifty out? Damn it's hot! I shouldn't have packed up all of my shorts."

I get so happy when it's sunny out. Except if I drank the night before.

Every March, I get excited for good weather because of the phrase about March coming in like a lion and out like a lamb. But when you're in the Northeast, the phrase should be "In like a lion, having the lion hang out for a while, and out like a slightly less ferocious lion."

The weirdest climate is the one you create in your dorm when you're heater is on too high so you sit by your open window while it's snowing. And instead of finding the middle ground of temperatures, you become the McBLT in those old commercials, with your hot side hot, your cool side cool, and your buns a bit too soggy to be comfortable.

Being Sick

Someone once asked me why I get sick so often. I downed my shot, pushed my beer away, finished my pizza, and told him I had no idea.

The people at health services think that the same thing causes every illness. "What's that? You have a fever, the sniffles, and you say you have a craving for chicken soup? Have you been having sex?"

If you start to doubt your relationship, all you have to do is come down with a cold. If your girlfriend or boyfriend shows up with chicken soup and a rented movie, you're fine. If they say "give me a call when you're feeling better," I'd put the folks from "Temptation Island" on speed dial.

Every semester, I get knocked out for a few days, but my professors are never too sick to make it to class. Doctorates must come with a life-time supply of Sudafed and a three-pound box of Kleenex.

Do you have a friend who has to blame someone whenever they get sick? "Dammit Steve, you had a cold last week. I must have caught it from you." Yeah, I guess I shouldn't have used your pillow as a handkerchief and ground my wet tissues into your eggs. My bad.

A friend of mine yelled at me for breathing too loud near him, but apologized the next day and explained that he was just sick. Sorry, but I don't think there's such thing as twenty-four-hour Turret's syndrome.

Campus health services to real doctors is like Columbia football is to the NFL. Sure people on Columbia's football team can play better football than I can, but I'm only going to the game cause it's free.

It's amazing how good you feel the first day your head clears after a cold. You wake up and you can suddenly breath again. Nothing makes you appreciate life like having seen it through watery eyes.

A nurse, before she gave me a shot, asked me where I wanted the needle. Now, I'm no medical expert, but shouldn't she be, well, a medical expert? Put it where it hurts the least and is most effective. If that spot doesn't exist, then put it away.

Travel

How come when you visit other schools, you look for people you know?

At one point, you will decide that you and a friend will take a bus half way across the country over break to visit some friends. The trip will totally be worth it - who wouldn't want to spend ten hours on a Greyhound to go to Ohio and see someone you'll see in a month anyway?

Here's a tip - NEVER fly back home the morning after the last day of finals. If you think fighting a vicious hangover on one hour of sleep was bad in your dorm room, try doing it at 20,000 feet.

When you get to a new campus, everything looks strange. The buildings are arranged differently, the system of signing in guests is unusual (if it's even there), and the dining halls are so confusing that you can't even get a piece of pizza. But if you pay attention, everyone is still listening to Dave Matthews, everyone is still talking about hooking up, and everyone still has that Animal House poster of John Belushi where his shirt just says "College." Home, sweet drunken home.

If I had one piece of advice for anyone in high school, it's to pretend you don't know how to drive while you're in college. My friends tell me that being able to drive gives them freedom. But I can drink when we go to bars and sleep during road trips. Who is the free one now?

It's funny how a car of guys will call out their window to a car of girls. What is supposed to happen? "Wow, we were driving on this highway all day wondering if any guys would yell to us. Some did, but they just didn't holler as loud as you. Since we are so impressed with your yelling ability, can we pull over, switch cars so there are an equal number of guys and girls in each, and drive wherever you're going? Please?"

Some cars come with TVs, fold-away seats, speaker phones, ten CD changers, and satellite-guided computer systems. But not one comes with a way to get rid of your empty cups and wrappers. I swear I'll invent the first car tailored for road trips. "The Ford Explorer: College Edition. Now with passenger-side steering, eight cup holders, no seat belts, and driver-side trash bags."

When you go to another school for a weekend, going out is a *lot* of fun. Walk into any bar, walk over to anyone, and say "what's the scene at this bar like?" When they ask why you want to know, tell them you're from another school, and if that doesn't start a conversation, tell them they're dumb and ugly. Either you'll have a conversation or you won't care because you'll never see them again. And you'll have a great story to start another conversation with when you get back to school.

It's annoying to have to compare stuff on other campuses to stuff at your own school. Almost annoying as walking around school with a friend as he compares everything to how it is at his campus.

Some schools are great, but no school is the best at everything. At Harvard, you may like your social scene. But telling a Florida State guy that you have better parties is like someone from Bumpkin Community College bragging to you about their astrophysics department.

I had a ticket once with a stop over, but wanted to cancel the first leg and drive instead. So they charged me extra because they said my cancellation made them lose money. Oh, I see - by returning something valuable and asking for no money back, I must have hurt you financially. And you wonder why airlines go out of business so often.

In some upper class hotels, they leave two bottles of water in every room, and you owe five dollars if you drink them. Which is so enticing - considering the bottled water is both warm *and* next to the sink.

When you get directions online, there's a warning that says "it's a good idea to check and make sure the road still exists." You're laughing now, but what an embarrassing way to die. You drive off a cliff, and at your funeral everyone says you should have listened to Yahoo.

I was staying at a hotel, and housekeeping asked me if I needed a new towel. Yes, I've been here for one night, and I've used all seventeen towels. I am Jo-Jo, the sweating boy. Wrap me in absorbent terrycloth.

College travel prepares you for anything beyond college. As long as it isn't a car filled with six guys, a dozen McDonalds wrappers, and five empty cases of Natty Ice, who cares if the airline is out of peanuts?

Glasses

I find it funny when some people don't recognize me without my glasses. After graduation, I bet they'll all find cushy jobs at the Daily Planet.

When I put contacts in for the first time, it took me forever because I kept blinking. So I got help from the woman whose only job was to teach people how to put in contacts. "No, no," she said, "you're not supposed to blink." Thanks ma'am - I hadn't thought of that.

Are you one of those people who try to pull off sunglasses indoors? Sure, you forgot you were wearing them. For the last hour. In class.

I've discovered that walking around without my glasses is an excellent way to ignore people I don't want to talk to. A few days later, they tell me that they passed by me and I didn't say hi. "Oh!," I say, apologetically. "I must not have been wearing my glasses. And I hate you."

I want to get corrective laser surgery instead of contacts or glasses. But I'm waiting five, ten, even fifteen years to make sure it's perfected. The last thing I want is for some crazy side effect a few years down the road. "Well Mr. Hofstetter, your vision appears to be fine, but we're really going to have to do something about this third nipple."

The idea of smart people wearing glasses comes from their vision being bad from reading so often. So if you're illiterate, can you see through walls? Because yeah, you couldn't read, but man it'd be cool to see through walls.

Wearing bifocals would help if you were dating someone with a great upper body but really fat legs.

I haven't been wearing my glasses as often as I used to. As much as I like seeing better, I hate looking worse.

You know what is really cool? Angst. You know what is even cooler? Thick black, non-prescription glasses to compliment your angst. You know what's the coolest? It's a tie between sarcasm and making fun of angsty people.

CHAPTER 4

THE SOCIAL LIFE

"It's sorta social. Demented and sad, but social."
-John Bender, The Breakfast Club

This quote, originally used to describe Brian Johnson's membership in the Physics Club, could easily describe half the recreational institutions in school. Study breaks. Intramural quiz bowl teams. A capella groups. All of them demented and sad, but social.

But this quote was appropriately uttered in a library, the most demented and sad social scene of all. Libraries are where stressed out kids go to meet stressed out kids, and not get any work done. See, if they actually did their work, they wouldn't be able to complain about how stressed they were anymore and would have nothing to talk about.

So college students, holding the kind of entrepreneurial spirit only found in poor young people and sports agents, have turned to other means of socializing. They meet people, they throw parties, they go to bars, and they participate in Greek life.

Many people think that the reason anyone is in Greek life is to consume alcohol. Untrue – that's the reason anyone is in *college*. While they're in college, kids drink – face it, it happens. But if you're in a fraternity or sorority, at least you've got a lot of people there to make sure you get home alive.

And Greek life is much more than just a social atmosphere. Greeks do things like tutor each other, run community service events, and participate in intramural and varsity sports. But there is no denying that joining a Greek organization will help your social life. Say you have fifty brothers or sisters, who you're already tight with. Each of them has friends you haven't otherwise met, and they have friends, and so on and so forth. It's amazing to meet that many people that you have yet to alienate. And being in a fraternity that throws a party instead of just attending the party is the difference between being the guy who knows the bouncer and actually being the bouncer.

You can have a social life without being Greek. You just have to be better at planning it. Or you go the way of Brian Johnson and join an academic club. Which to dorks like him, are social.

Friends

The best part of visiting friends is the pictures their parents have on their wall. Sure, you're an Abercrombie shopping, white baseball cap-wearing stud now, but what did you look like at your Bar Mitzvah?

If you find yourself constantly apologizing for one of your friends, start making fun of them instead. Now, someone else can apologize to you!

Every girl eventually has an asshole guy friend - the guy that was interested in her at some point but took a wrong turn, and now other guys have to impress him. Some people look for girls that don't have an asshole guy friend. But I wouldn't recommend it - it might seem nice for her not to have one at the time, but that means the job is still open.

Every group of friends has a lowest section of the totem poll - you know, the person they usually make fun of and is only really there for the pure entertainment value. The next time you go out with your friends, look around for a few minutes - and pray you can figure out who it is.

Not everyone is from your hometown. When I'm visiting, my friends say stuff like, "Let's hit the strip tonight" or "Poochie is having a party over on Collins" or "Wanna go to the walk and get a Mac Dog?" Sure. As long as one comes with a map to what the hell you just said.

I never know what to call my friends' parents when I meet them. Sure, I'm twenty-two. Yes, I'm on a first name basis with many people older than they are. But when someone lays out a sleeping bag for me, gives me the extra family towels, and cooks me breakfast lunch and dinner before asking when we're going to get the car back that night, referring to them as Herb and Judy just seems wrong.

It's fun to see a friend interacting with his parents. Because it's fun to think that it's the same guy who puked all over his roommate last week.

Some people in college are your constant acquaintances. They're in your lit class, you have a mutual friend, or maybe they were on your hall freshman year. But every once in a while, they'll be your closest friend - when they see you in a bar talking to someone they think is hot.

Greek Life

I don't understand why people don't rush. I mean, if there's one thing I hate, it's getting free stuff while meeting people.

Do you have a friend who looks for Greek letters in movies, just so he can try to identify the fraternity? This is the same guy who calls 867-5309 and gets pissed when Jenny doesn't answer.

Someone was trying to explain to me why rushing was a bad idea. Now this would be fine if I were thinking of rushing, but I'm *running* rush. Think about what you're saying. "I think anyone who buys a Dave Matthews CD is an idiot. By the way, Mr. Matthews, how are you?"

Sorority rush and fraternity rush are completely different. Sorority rush involves visits to all the houses, and bid lists, and preferences, and complex rules about who you can and can't talk to and for how long. Fraternity rush involves nachos and college football.

Some sororities send clear messages during rush. They say, "we value you for who you are, we don't want to change you, we value your individuality, and we are all unique." And they say it with their fifty sisters all dressed in black pants, black sandals, and white baby tees.

It's weird when everyone in a sorority dresses the same during rush as a symbol of unity. Unless they're wearing bikinis. Then it's pretty cool.

In most schools, if you're in a fraternity, you meet twice as many people as you would otherwise. I told that to someone once and they said, "yeah, but they're all Greeks." Yeah, jerk, so am I.

Schools hold Greek organizations to a higher standard than other clubs when it comes to alcohol. If someone in a fraternity drinks themselves sick, every one of their brothers gets punished, even if it happened half way across the world. Is it like this in any other campus organization? "A young man was rushed to the hospital after consuming five times the legal limit of alcohol. In response, the University has suspended the charter of his a cappella group, shut down the sixth floor of the freshman dorm, and barred anyone from becoming a bio major again."

Parties

I love the guy who yells "party!" at the top of his lungs. Beer, dim lighting, a couple going at it in the corner - I could have sworn I was in class. Thanks for clearing that up.

Your school's level of parties is directly proportional to how good your teams are, and there's no good reason why. When ten guys are really good at basketball, everyone else just drinks, dances, and hooks up a lot more. Even during football season.

I'm amazed at the stupidity of college administrators when it comes to alcohol. At a university-sponsored party, you need two IDs to drink, but they don't necessarily have to have the same name or face on them.

People think that if they drink a lot at a party, they'll be cool, which is not always true. If you drink a lot and can hold it, that's cool. If you drink just enough to leave you passed out in your own puke, well, not as cool.

Formals are just college parties with people dressed nicer. You still chug, you still play drinking games, there's one couple making out half way through it - but you know what really keeps it classy? Suits.

When you leave a party at 5:00 AM, no matter how important that call to your girlfriend seems at the time, just let it go. She'll still be there tomorrow. Well, only if you don't call her now.

People prefer parties that are numbered. House Party 3. Big Jam 7. It might be the first time we throw a party, but my fraternity will call it number 28 anyway. We've heard too many first-semester freshmen say, "we can't miss this party man, it's a tradition" not to capitalize on it.

Some people are only comfortable at parties if they are on their way somewhere. You know the guy - he gets a drink, goes to the bathroom, walks outside to smoke, checks his voicemail. Sure, he looks important. But by the end of the night, he's had fifteen drinks, peed a dozen times, and smoked a pack of cigarettes, yet somehow missed the reason he doesn't have voicemail is that he's never actually talked to anyone.

Smoking

I've been a smoker for four years. I've never touched a cigarette, but if you go to a college bar and breathe, you're a smoker.

Some people say they're social smokers because they only smoke in social situations. It's impressive that these people can find a pack a day worth of social situations.

A friend of mine only smokes when she sees her parents. Which would be fine if she didn't live with them.

I knew a guy who said he wasn't a smoker since he never paid for cigarettes. He never paid for lunch either but I never saw him go hungry.

I went into one of those walk-in freezer rooms at a grocery store with a friend of mine, and she wasn't cold at all. Then I realized that this is the same girl who wears pajamas outside in a snowstorm just to have a few puffs of a cigarette.

Imagine if other illegal things smelled as strongly as pot. "Hey, do you smell armed robbery?" "Yeah. It's the guy at the end of the hall." "Man, the least he can do when he's robbing a bank is close his damn door."

There's a difference between pot as a recreation and as a lifestyle. It's a recreation when you hear your friend mention it every few weeks. It's a lifestyle when people think your friend's first name is "do you smoke?"

Coffee shops sell magazines. Bagel stores sell orange juice. Shoe stores sell socks. Why don't drug dealers sell Doritos?

I told a friend of mine he looked stoned, and he asked how I knew. It wasn't the glassy eyes or the goofy expression on his face - it was the fact that he spent the last half hour saying "dude, I am so f-ing stoned!"

I guess pot makes people nicer. I'm constantly hearing people say "Hey, you want some pot?" Does this happen with anything else that expensive? "Hey, I just bought a bunch of caviar. You want some? If you like it, I know where you can get more."

Bars

Twenty-one is such an arbitrary age to be allowed to drink. Especially when you consider that you can be tried as an adult much earlier. Though that law probably cuts down on the "your honor, I was, like, totally smashed" defense.

Fake IDs are not made to fool bouncers - they're made to be good enough for the bouncers to decide to allow you in. These guys know that anything with evidence of a printer, nail polish, or a holographic key is a fake. They also know that they have no job unless you drink.

A friend of mine who had already turned twenty-one was pissed at me once because I got carded. Yeah, it's my fault that I was born so late in the year. Sorry, my parents should have had sex a few months earlier. I guess they're just late for everything.

People think that something magical will happen at bars. That for some reason, the cute girl that ignores them the whole year will see them at a bar and think they're cool because of it. So everyone spends seventy bucks on a fake and spends ten minutes trying to convince the bouncer that the reason that the ID is crumbling and see-through is cause it's "the old kind." So everyone finally gets into the bar, except that one friend who looks twelve that doesn't even need to get in the bar cause he has a girlfriend, and you sit around a table playing quarters.

Getting a family member's old license is cool if you look anything like them. But if you're a 6'4 blonde, do not try to use your 5'6" brunette brother's ID. Betty White and Barry White have the same last name too, but you don't see them passing for each other.

Never argue with a bouncer about your fake ID. You were caught. You're done. Go home. Do you think acting indignant will get you in? That's like your credit card company calling because your bill is three months late and you saying "Dude, the check is really, really in the mail."

Using an "international student" fake ID to get into a bar is the second biggest scam there is. The biggest is the guy who pocketed sixty bucks selling you an ID that'll never work.

If politicians want to commend someone for family values, they should give a medal to the skeezy middle-aged man at the end of the bar who hits on all your underaged friends. The abject fear of becoming him is what convinces most big players to finally settle down and raise a family.

Paying twenty bucks for a bad fake ID is like buying half a pair of pants. You really need the whole thing to be let in anywhere.

Who is the genius who made darts into a bar game? "My depth perception is severely impaired, but I'd enjoy some sort of game. I got it! I'll throw sharp things in a cramped space!" This is the same guy who thought of drive through liquor stores and put brail on car manuals.

Why are some girls still surprised when guys approach them at bars? It's a bar. That's what guys do at bars. If you don't want to talk to anyone, stay in your room and instant message your friends about how skeezy guys tried to talk to you at the bar last night.

If you don't have any other place than a dorm to hang out in, okay. But guess what - if you live off campus, you can go to the supermarket, buy a few cases of beer for the price of a pitcher, and come back to an ID free environment where if you drink too much you can fall asleep without getting pickpocketed. Of course, then that hot girl can't come over and start talking to you, right?

The Five Main Types of Campus Bars
A Public Service From Student Body Shots

The Freshman Bar: Where the carding is easy, the beer is easier, and the girls are the easiest.
The Jock Bar: Where campus athletes and girls in tube tops convene. Occassionally, the athletes will assert their rights to the bar and the tube tops by throwing ice at the other patrons.
The Has-been Bar: This bar used to be cool before it started attracting all of the alumni who remembered it as cool. Then it just became sketchy and old.
The Club: Where college students pay a $20 cover to buy $8 beer.
The Trendy Bar: The drink specials here are slightly more expensive than the regular drinks at the jock bar. These only last for a year, when their lease expires and they become the has-been bar.

Alcohol

If warm Budweiser tastes like piss, does cold piss taste like Budweiser? Because man, I could use the money.

The kids who really drank in high school had fakes when they were sixteen that said they were twenty-one. So now they're a sophomore and their ID says they're twenty-four, but the proctors at university sponsored parties don't realize the problem. Here's a tip - in the first few months of a year, maybe 30% of the campus is twenty-one and half of them won't be there since they're either burnt out from partying since freshman year or never partied at all. Anyone under twenty-one should be glad colleges don't do math.

Colleges don't want you to drink in your room, and they say it's because of safety. They'd prefer you get smashed at a bar, only to drive home and stumble across campus drunk, falling several times on the way and laughing about how funny it is that you're cut up and bruised, eventually trying to get past your guard and RA reeking of alcohol without them noticing, and crash in your bed. If you could drink in your room, then you could just get smashed and go to sleep. But safety first.

You know you have a drinking problem when the bartender tells you to call ahead if you can't make it so he doesn't worry.

When you first come to college, beer paraphernalia is very cool, and so you collect all of it that you can. But by graduation, it sort of wears off, and you're left with three happy hour banners, a bag full of coasters, eight pint glasses that you stole from a bar, four promotional pins that used to blink, and three dozen empty beer bottles. But don't throw it away. Give it to a freshman who, for the next four years, will think beer paraphernalia is very cool.

When they pour your drink before you order, you're a regular. But when they set up your drinking game for you, it's time to take a night off.

I talk to my friends the next day after a bad night of drinking and they say the college student's mantra: "I will never drink again." I've learned that in college, the word "again" really means "til Thursday."

Would Mexico's economy be better if they could charge $5 for a Corona?

The second worst thing is to wake up after a long night of drinking and see vomit on your floor. The worst thing is to realize that it's not yours.

When you come back drunk, for godsakes, do not check your e-mail. And if by some chance you do, never hit "reply to all".

After 2:00 AM on a weekend, Instant Messenger should have a sobriety test. If you come home and can't type "I'm not saying this because I'm drunk, I really think you should come over" with less than three mistakes, it'd be better off for everyone if you just went to sleep.

Passing out on your bed with a high blood alcohol level is nothing. Waking up the next day still legally drunk - now that's impressive.

In drinking games, one person wins and the other drinks. It's the only kind of game I've ever heard of that makes both sides happy.

A guy needs to be good at four things. The three standards are poker, pool, and darts. The fourth could either be drinking games or aiming your vomit, but you have to have talent at one of them.

Watching a baseball game and drinking whenever someone scores is okay. Doing it for a basketball game is not.

No one ever turns down free beer. You could be drunk, on medication, throwing up, and allergic to hops. You know what else you are? Poor.

There are two types of girls in college: girls who don't drink beer, and girls who do keg stands.

Politicians call five or more beers in one sitting binge drinking. I know some people who call it breakfast.

If you go to the website of any beer company, they ask your birthday to validate your age. I'm looking forward to the technology that allows you to hold your ID up to the screen while avoiding eye contact and pretending to be involved in a conversation with the guy next to you.

CHAPTER 5
MEN AND WOMEN

If any guy out there thinks he truly understands women, you should write a book about them. Then when a girl rejects you, you can flip out and shoot twelve people from a water tower before showing the book to the judge and pleading insanity.

"What? You thought you understood women? No one understands women! Case dismissed!"

Women don't understand men either. But I can't understand why not. Men are simple creatures who like fire, meat, sex, and combat. Sometimes a guy will be able to have sex after playing football at a barbecue, and the whole world will seem at peace.

Actually, gay men don't understand men, and gay women don't understand women either. See, men don't understand anyone, even other men, and no one, even other women, can understand a woman.

It is, however, men basing their lives on these four things that allow women to trick us into dating. Going to a fancy restaurant and ordering a steak knocks the first two out of the way. And in order to achieve sex, guys must combat the impressions of every guy a girl has ever dated. It's a pretty solid system. And what it all boils down to is the survival instinct. Fire creates heat, meat represents nourishment, sex creates other men, and combat eliminates the weak ones. Survival.

The majority of what I understand about women involves their complete and utter dominance over men. The ability to make us walk them home, move their bookshelves, fix their computers, or do just about anything else simply by wearing a tube top. Imagine if men could wield that kind of power with just one piece of cotton and spandex.

Men are constantly chasing women, which shows that women really hold the control. If the hunter held the power, there would be no hunt. Face it guys, it's only when they get tired of running that we feel we've caught anything. But hooking up with a college girl is kind of like Elmer Fudd catching Bugs Bunny. As happy as you briefly are, it was only because your prey slowed down to laugh at you. And by the time you open your eyes, you'll be alone in the woods in a funny hat.

Men and women, please go to your corners, and come out swinging. I want a good clean fight. Let's get it on!

Interaction

Some girl I met at a bar told me that she wanted my friend, and I wasn't supposed to tell him. That's like laughing with the secret service about how you're going to kill the president.

When I was in high school, I was told that when I got to college, girls would stop falling for jerks. When I was a freshman in college, I was told that towards the end of college, girls would stop falling for jerks. Towards the end of college, I was told that after college, girls would stop falling for jerks. Apparently, no matter how old you get, jerks are still very good looking.

The winter is tough on looks - everyone is bundled up, people put on a few pounds, and they all get way too pale. If you think someone still looks good during the winter, marry them before the weather gets warm again and you miss your chance.

God has played a number of cruel jokes in his time. But the cruelest is that when females live together, their cycles coincide. So what happens at school? You fill a hallway full of them, and then mix in exams, papers, and your standard social pressures. But that's not a recipe for disaster.

A guy stepping into the middle of a girl conversation is always awkward. You sit down at a table with a few girls you know, and you ask if you could move your friend's purse so you can have a place to eat. And someone says, "Oh, that's a great bag, where'd you get that?" And then everyone is talking about Prada and Kate Spade and Fendi. And it's all your fault.

I'm pretty sure at one point or another, every guy has had a girl turn to them and say , "I'm really glad that we can be such good friends and talk like this." And no matter how hard we try, she will never say follow that with "but it'd be even better if we could talk like this, *and* have sex."

How many guys have ever heard a hot girl complain that she can't get guys? That's not true - you can get guys, you just can't get *nice* guys. You know why? Because instead of flirting with them, you spend all your time together talking about how you can't get guys.

Differences

Girls and guys punctuate their anger differently. Girls can blame PMS for being upset, and it's just accepted that guys are assholes. So girls can blame their period, while guys can blame their colon.

I heard someone say, "boys will be boys." Good - otherwise, they'd have been named wrong.

Guys have a complex system of dibs. If a girl is your first dibs, then none of your boys can touch her. If she's your second dibs, then it'd be nice for your boys to lay off, but it's acceptable if they don't. Girls have a simpler system - backstabbing each other and then telling everyone that the guy is a prick for hooking up with both of you.

No matter how important they are to girls, guys do not look at shoes. And even if we do, we do not know the difference between Jimmy Choos and Manalo Blahniks. I hadn't even heard of those until I asked someone for names of women's shoes to complete that sentence.

Men and women come home drunk differently. Women will perk up suddenly, yell about how much fun they had at the bar, and then stumble into a wall or fall on the floor, laughing hysterically about how they can take care of themselves. Guys will perk up suddenly, fight off their friend that is holding them up, and then stumble into a wall or fall on the floor trying to take a swing, shouting something about how they can take care of themselves. The next day, neither will have any idea how the guard possibly knew they were drunk.

Guys don't talk about what they did with a girl. A guy will come home, and his friend will say, "so, did you?" And the guy will say "yeah" and maybe even a number to signify how many times. A girl gets back, and proceeds to tell her girlfriends what he wore, everything he said, how much the take-out food cost, and exactly what he did with his tongue.

Nine times out of ten, if a reasonably attractive girl were to approach a guy at a bar and say "will you walk me home," he will. Nine times out of ten, if a reasonably attractive guy were to approach a girl at a bar and say "will you walk me," he'll get ignored by the time he says "home."

College girls go for the Ken doll type - he looks nice, he has plastic hair, and he's got absolutely nothing on the inside. College guys go for the Pez dispenser type - their bodies are pretty much all the same, and though most men would prefer a Princess Leah head over a Miss Piggy, the guy usually only cares about the candy below the neck.

When guys lose weight, they like hearing about it. When girls lose weight, you can tell them they look incredible, but you can't say why. I told a friend of mine that she looked like she lost ten pounds. So of course that meant I was saying she was fat and ugly before.

Girls say "Oh, I hate her, she's so pretty." You will never hear guys say anything like that about other guys. Guys try to make friends with good-looking guys because guys can do people-math. If ten girls want the same guy, some of them are going to have to be distracted.

Women get dressed slightly differently than men. Women hold their clothes up to their body, while men hold their clothes up to their nose.

Girls - guys will not tell you if they like your haircut. Half the time they try, it turns out that you just combed it differently, and the guy looks dumb for suggesting it was cut when it wasn't. Guys - girls do not care about how well you did in that intramural basketball game. So what if you scored twenty points, you were playing against the women's chess team. Get over yourself, and compliment her haircut.

Did you know that girls are all part of a vast network of spies? When a guy likes a girl, his friends might mention if they saw her talking to another guy. When a girl has a crush on someone, her friends memorize his class schedule, know where he ate lunch, and call her every time they see someone who has the same jacket.

Girls ask if they look fat. Guys rub their growing beer gut with pride.

Lets face it: guys are dumb and girls are crazy. Girls do irrational things for no apparent reason and then expect you to know why, and refuse to apologize for it. But even knowing and accepting that, I still do things that I know will set someone off. Why? Because I'm a guy, and guys are dumb. See how this works?

Hooking Up

Waking up with someone you care about is great. Except if you're hungover and they're waking up for an 8:00 AM class. Then it sucks.

Hooking up with someone for the first time can be unnerving because everybody has their own style. And no matter how well things are going, you can never say "the last person I was with really liked me to do this swirly thing with my tongue. How about you?"

Do you know what a DUFF is? Guys do. It's a Designated Ugly Fat Friend that hot girls have to boost their self-confidence and test a guy. The DUFF tries to intercept you, and the hot girl subconsciously sees how you interact with her. But it's okay because guys have their own secret weapon: their buddy with a girlfriend who can distract the DUFF while you continue the conversation. We don't have a short nickname for him, just "the guy that takes one for the team."

Midterms make hookups simple, because the only two things open after midnight are bars and campus libraries. All you have to do is decide whether you want someone to forget you the next day because they were too drunk or too stressed, and you'll know where to go.

When you hookup with someone in a bar, you don't know how to treat them the next day, when you're not drunk. Sometimes, you totally snub them - walking right by without even smiling. But odds are you'll see them in a bar the next weekend and be able to apologize. "Look, I'm really sorry for my behavior the other day. I must have been sober. I hope you understand I just wasn't myself."

I never say someone's name when I'm hooking up with them. Not because I'm afraid of getting it wrong, but because I think it's weird when someone says mine. Even if I'm fooling around, when someone says, "Steve," it's just instinctive for me to answer with, "what?"

There are some guys who try stuff and see if they get slapped. But most of us will brush up against things to gauge the reaction. That way if the girl is like "what are you doing?," we can just pretend it was an accident that the back of our hand landed squarely between her thighs.

Dating

Meeting the parents is the second biggest step in a college relationship. Actually going on a date instead of spending all your time together in one of your rooms - now that's big.

My friends agreed that they each get to pick one celebrity that, if the chance arose, they'd be allowed to cheat with. That could get dangerous when "celebrity" turns into "kid in my lit class."

You know plenty of people who came to school freshman year with a boyfriend or girlfriend from "back home." How many of those couples lasted past Thanksgiving? A few last til January, but that's only for the sake of their "we'll always be together" ad in the high school yearbook.

No one dates in college. Instead, the guy asks the girl to watch TV in his lounge, so he can show her off to all his friends and maybe hook up with her in his room later. The girl asks the guy to sit in her room while she rearranges her desk and shows him pictures of people from high school that she doesn't even talk to anymore, so she can show him off to her friends, and turn him down when he tries to hook up with her.

When your girlfriend makes you watch N*SYNC, it's not so bad. When she tells all of your friends about it, that's pretty bad.

Senior year, some of your friends start asking you if you're going to get married. Yeah, the happy couple is registered for a six of Beast, a lovely set of Red Hook pint glasses, and half a bottle of Jack.

No offense to anyone, but if you don't date much in college, then you won't date much after college. Think of the situation you've been given. You live in a one-mile area that consists of thousands of members of the opposite sex, 99% of whom aren't married, and all within four years of your age. If that's not enough, you're put in small rooms with these people for four months, and you're given a new set of people for the next four months - and this happens eight times. No one has an unlisted phone number, and everyone eats in the same place. Members of the opposite sex are given a lot of alcohol, and are all hanging out in the same five places every night. Face it, if you can't score now, give up.

The Bases

The first thing you really need to understand is that guys are hitting and girls are pitching. If guys were pitching, batting averages would be upwards of .900, ERAs would be in double digits, and major league baseball would shatter its record for home runs in a single season.

When we were in high school, there were four bases. A French kiss was a single, up the shirt was a double, down the pants was a triple, and sex was obviously scoring. But college is to high school what major league baseball is to little league. There are still four bases, but how many little leaguers can hit seventy-three home runs?

You'd be amazed just how descriptive the baseball metaphor can get. Sure, you know the four bases, but was the double a head first slide? Was that triple hit at a home game or an away game? Have you ever hit a single and gotten thrown out trying to steal second by the catcher with a quick arm? Don't pretend you didn't understand all of that.

A walk is when the girl hands you first base, and you don't even have to put the ball in play to get there (though a walk is as good as a hit). A sacrifice happens if you purposely get yourself out simply to advance a teammate. Stealing involves moving up more than one base at a time. And if you remember your little league days, the home team gets to bat last - or in baseball terms, "last licks."

A friend of mine once told me that he had fooled around with the only girl he ever asked out, and thus he was batting 1.000. I told him that in his only at-bat with the Indians, Jamie Quirk hit a home run, leaving him with a 1.000 batting average, and a 4.000 slugging percentage. My friend asked me who the hell Jamie Quirk was. I said, "exactly."

Some people have very different definitions of what the bases are. Which is okay, but once they start playing with the rest of us, they're going to have to learn the rules or face a possible suspension.

Good ballplayers want to face the best pitcher in the league. If you hit a home run off of some guy on the Devil Rays, who cares? I'll take a K against a Cy Young over a home run off of a middle-reliever any day.

Rejection

I almost used the "it's not you, it's me" line. But I'm sure it was her.

Some people decide that a relationship is going too fast, and they want to "take some time off." You know what that means in English? "I really like you, but I want to have sex with other people before we get married."

I don't understand when people break up and consciously decide to stay friends. Does this happen in any place else? "This is the toughest part of my job. I know you've been here for years, but we're cutting back around the office, and we're letting you go. But can you still come in and get me some coffee every once in while? I'd really like that."

Hey guys - next time you say "I really like you, but I can't handle a relationship," think of how dumb you sound. This is my loose translation: "You're too nice. I need a slut so when I cheat on her, she won't mind as much since she's doing the same thing."

I know a girl who laughed when she made out with someone. Right in the middle of it - just burst out laughing. And she did this with everyone she ever kissed. Or that's what I tell myself to keep the self-esteem up.

You know what "I just want to be friends" really means? It means "I'm too much of a weenie to tell the truth." If any guy tells you this and actually calls you, hangs out with you, and confides in you like any other friend, let me know. They haven't awarded this year's Nobel Prizes yet, and I think he's a contender.

Someone once told me that they couldn't date me because I was too smart. But by believing them, I instantly proved them wrong.

Everyone is entitled to some emotional baggage: no more than two items, small enough to stow under the seat in front of you.

Some people still use the line "We're too close of friends." This worked in high school, when no one understood human nature. But think about what you're saying. "Sorry, I only date guys that repulse me so much that I wouldn't even want to be friends with them." Now that's class.

CHAPTER 6

ACADEMICS

"I like school. It's just too bad classes get in the way."
-Zach Morris, Saved By The Bell

More than fifty pages about college, and I'm just getting to the reason we're *supposed* to be here. Some people enjoy classes, and I admit I have had some great ones. But most of us love it here *despite* our classes. Without the schoolwork, we're at Camp College, where you get to run around and play all day. As soon as you wake up.

When I started here, I was so indoctrinated by high school that I scheduled all of my classes in a row, starting at 10AM. Sure, I was done by mid afternoon, but then I sat at my computer and did nothing. When you have 10 hours to do your homework, you can only concentrate for a half hour. But if you start your whole day later and schedule breaks in between classes and have to get your work done, you'll finish everything and have time to go out that night. Which you can do, since you don't have to wake up until noon anyway.

For lecture classes, I find that if I do the reading the day after class, I actually learn a lot better. See, if you haven't done the reading yet, you're forced to take notes in class. And when you take notes, you don't tune out, so you're actually listening the whole time (and you get the benefit of learning what the teacher thinks is important). Then when you finally do the reading, you actually understand it, having already internalized the general points in class. When it's time for the final, you've got intricate notes and a basic comprehension of what's going on before you even sit down to study. For seminars and workshops, you should just study psychoanalysis. Then whenever you're called on, you'll know a billion different ways to say, "well, what do you think?"

If you can, try to take all of your seminars and workshops during your senior year. Those classes usually come without finals, and when you're crying about how you have no job, you will be able to wipe your tears with something other than an exam with a big F on it.

Whether or not you want to wake up in the morning, before or after your alarm gives out a warning, you will never make it on time. But you will grab your books – after all, part of college is the academics.

Registration

One professor wouldn't let me in his class because I missed the first day. Little did he know that I had originally planned on missing much more than that.

On the first day of one of my classes, the department chair read out a list of the first eighteen people to sign up and told everyone else to leave. I spent the next hour in the hall arguing my way back into class until she finally told me that she'd have let me in, but I had already missed the first class, and therefore couldn't catch up on the work. Then she cackled heartily and retreated back to the cave of irony.

My campus didn't have computer registration until my senior year. Before then, we were supposed to register by phone, but only after we used our bare feet to peddle our bronto-mobile over to the rock quarry.

The best day you will ever experience in college is not your first party, it's not when you hook up with that really hot girl/guy you've been chasing for two years, and it's not when you graduate. The best day is when you're sitting in class the second semester of your senior year, and your teacher passes out next semester's course guide.

All of Coulmbia's classes start with 1001 instead of 101. We're no good at football, but we're great at pretending that we're ten times smarter than everyone else.

At some schools, students are allowed to "shop around" during the first week or two of class to decide which sections they want to be in. Why don't they save time and just tell us how many hot girls there are?

I know some people who go to fifteen classes the first week to find the easiest ones. Obviously not math classes. Because they've just spent twelve hours that week trying to get out of about ten hours of work.

At Columbia, you can shop around for classes, but you can only register for five during pre-registration. You spend the first week of school deciding exactly which classes you want, and the next week forgetting about them because they've been full since July.

Books

I was upset at my bookstore for paying me so little for my used books. I'd hardly call anything still shrink-wrapped in cellophane "used."

I had an economics professor who assigns $200 worth of books to 400 students twice a year. If she really knew anything about economics, she'd have opened her own bookstore.

Some professors assign one main book and list the rest as "suggested reading." Except there is no such thing as "suggested reading." What your teacher means is "this is the crap that will be on the test that you'll forget to study. Remember not to read it when you get the chance."

How cool would it be if there were a book just of important terms, people, and places for each subject? And you know you'd still read only the last page of each chapter.

When you really hate a book that you have to read for class, you want to be the brilliant and daring kid who is the first to admit that they didn't agree with the reading. Until the professor tells you that her dad wrote it.

You can't use Cliffs Notes for contemporary novels. But I'm kind of curious if I'm the only one who still doesn't read the book and checks the Amazon.com user feedback instead.

All of the history and English majors I know kept most of their books after graduation, but none of my friends in any of the sciences did. I'm not sure if that's because history books can be translated more easily to post-college life, or because science books cost $100 a piece.

If my professor gives out 200 pages of reading, I'll only do the first fifty and wonder why he assigned so much. So the next week he gives fifty pages. I read the first ten and wonder why they assigned so much.

Teachers that asign their own books is one of the more obnoxious things in college. "There's been some brilliant commentary written on this subject that I think you should all read. Mine!"

Studying

You can tell if someone likes you if they make sure to study with just you before a big exam. Especially if you're dumb.

To some, procrastination is an art. To some, it's a hobby. To me, it's a religion. "Welcome to the Church of Our Lady of Perpetual Procrastination. Services will be held five minutes after I'm done writing my sermon, and complimentary Jolt Cola will be served. Take your seat in the back of the chapel, and leave an IOU in the collection plate."

I can't stay up all night to study. When I'm that tired, I don't have trouble picking a,b,c, or d. Just remembering what order they come in.

When you try to comfort someone studying, don't ever do it by saying, "don't worry, it'll all be over in a few days." They'll ignore "it'll all be over" and just hear "in a few days" before they breakdown crying.

My mom told me if I spent half as much time studying as I did on baseball, I'd be a straight A student. "You get a B in history, but you can tell me Keith Miller's batting average from 1987." I said, ".373, though he didn't have enough at bats to qualify for the batting title so Tony Gwynn won with a .370—but that's completely besides the point."

Everyone looks for a better place to study. During the semester, there is ample space, but every nook of every building is used during finals. Except your teacher's office during office hours - that's still empty.

I'm going to rent myself out as a curve-straightener. For just fifty bucks, I'll find the smartest three kids in your class and continuously poke them in them the forehead until they can't remember a damn thing.

After I study, I feel like the guy in Flowers for Algernon. I know I have twenty-four hours to be smart before I forget everything. Or at least I think that's what happened - I haven't read it in a few days.

I have an intricate system of studying. I prepare flashcards from my notes. I test myself on the material. I read the timelines in the book. I take notes on what I don't know. Then, I copy off the kid next to me.

Classes

What is the point of auditing a class? You sit through the lecture and take notes, but you don't have to pay for it. Which would make sense if professors charged at the door.

Why do some teachers try to teach on the first day? We're supposed to come in, they give us the syllabus, brag about what degrees they have, reminisce fondly about how they were an undergraduate forty years ago, make us fill out an index card, and say good-bye. After a month of watching TV and sleeping til 3:00, that's really all my brain can handle.

My class was talking with the professor once about how the reading started slow. Then one guy said that he got so bored by it that he stopped reading after a few pages. And that's where he lost the rest of us. Say you're at work and you take an hour coffee break. When your boss asks you how the coffee was, you can say, "good." You don't say, "Good. I had it instead of doing your stupid work, you horse's ass."

Why is it that some schools have the coolest majors? I know people who are majoring in things like "Radio Journalism" and "Constructing Foreign Policy" but I'm stuck with "History" or "English." I want to be a sports writer, and the only thing that came close was American History. And I can't even take just the good classes in that department because they force me to take classes "outside my concentration." Cause if I didn't, one day I'd write a column for my local sports section, and my glaring lack of East African history would be obvious to all my readers.

All my teachers say, "you need to know this so you can impress people at cocktail parties." Maybe there should be one required class called "boring crap you need to know for cocktail parties." Two weeks of music theory, a month of art history, one class on bio, one on anthropology, and one on how to trade stocks and shop online. The final is discussing wines and laughing pretentiously. If I'm ever at a party where I need to know math, physics, or a macro policy model, I'm leaving.

There are three types of people in this world - those who can count, those who can't, and those who think dumb math jokes are funny.

People declare majors so they'll have something to talk about in bars.

When you go out drinking during the week, people get in a war over how early their first class is. "I have a class at ten tomorrow!" "Oh yeah? I have a lab at nine!" "Oh yeah? I have class eight-thirty, and we have a final!" Not me - my earliest class of the week is at 2:00 PM and I'm proud. I'll try to wake you up for your final before I get to bed.

In history class, we were discussing how there were communists in every profession. And I wondered - if there really were communist mailmen, did they give the same amount of mail to everyone?

I try to take classes that overlap. I signed up for "Post-Civil War America," "America since World War II," and "America in the Fifties" in one semester. So I neglected my readings for several classes at once.

One of my writing professors said that in order to write about something, you have to live it. He recommended bungee jumping, hang gliding, cliff diving, and other things like that. But I think he's missing an important caveat : to write about something, you have to live through it.

I heard that more than 90% of everyone at Harvard graduates with honors. First I thought of how that defeated the purpose of honors. But then I thought about the poor schlub who didn't get them and I started wondering how it would feel to know you're the dumbest guy on the floor. But then I remembered that it's not so bad.

My friends study computers, architecture, and biology, but they all say they're engineers. But writers never say they're engineers. We can think of more than one word for "guy who designs stuff."

I was an English major for a bit, and everyone asked me if I intended to use that to work at McDonald's. Hey buddy, when's the last time you heard anyone at McDonald's speak English?

In some classes, I sit towards the left, in some the right, and in some, the middle. But in each class, I have one and only one seat. In one class, I tried to switch things and move up a row. Man, that was a weird day.

Midterms

What's the point of a midterm in a class where the final is cumulative? That way, you get to study the material all night, and forget all of it the next day - twice!

No one sees the true importance of midterms. You hardly study for it since the final is worth a whopping 40% of your grade and the midterm is only worth a paltry 35%.

I hate when professors have three different exams, and call them all midterms. Don't they understand what the "mid" refers to?

Remember midterms first semester freshman year, and how you thought they were the toughest thing you had ever faced in your entire life? Now do you see how easy they were?

A lot of professors can't add. My midterm was worth 35% of my grade once. My final was worth 40%, and two papers were 10% each. But that final 5% of my grade made sure I came to class and participated every single day, or I would have failed.

Bless the teachers who let you keep the midterm. Actually, bless the teachers who let your friend who already took the class keep the midterm.

When I want to go out with one my friends and he says he can't because he has a midterm the next day, I can respect that. But refusing on a Saturday night to stay in and study? Come on, stay out til four, wake up at 1:00, hang over til 3:00 - that gives you a solid nine hours of studying by the time you hit midnight.

I had a professor so dumb that we convinced her to drop the lowest grade on the midterms. It took her a week before she realized that that we only get one midterm.

I once had five midterms in two days, and when I told someone about it, they told me that they had six. Not only did I know they were only taking five classes, but apparently, math wasn't one of them.

Papers

Why do professors still say ten-fifteen pages? Why can't they just say nine pages with five lines on the tenth page?

I find that when I just ramble and accidentally arrive at a conclusion, I get a B+ or an A-. So sometimes I use note cards to meticulously plan out what I'm going to write in the most succinct way possible, and I usually get a B+ or an A-. But then I've also spent 79 cents on note cards so I feel better about myself.

Once, I actually completed a paper two days before it was due. Of course I thought I was handing it in five days late.

For the classes I have with finals, I fill up an entire notebook. For the classes I have that just have papers, the notebook has a bunch of half-drawn pictures, notes from the class we had before I realized there was no final, and the date crossed out each time I didn't take notes.

Plenty of people have written papers on books they've never read. But to write a paper on a book you've never even seen - that's the mark of a true professional.

Some people type in courier new or arial or change the margins or headings. But the best way to add a line here and there is to be wordy where it counts. Find paragraphs whose last line extends near the margin and play around with synonyms until one word falls on the next line. And then use courier new and extend the margins.

If you can only write what you know, how the heck have I written so many papers about stuff I've never heard of?

Getting caught plagiarizing is the dumbest thing I've ever heard of. With all these online translating services available now, translate the paper from English to German, then from German to French, and from French to English. Clean up the grammar, and it may as well be yours.

It takes me twenty minutes to write a two-page paper. But it took me four years to write a decent one.

Finals

Senior year, finals are different. They feel so, I don't know, final.

Finals are scheduled carefully. Universities coordinate a huge schedule based on complex algorithms of which students most often take which classes together, schedule the tests accordingly, and even write-in a provision where if you have too many finals in one day, you can postpone some. Midterms are scheduled consecutively on the same day with a space of three minutes between them.

The American Heritage dictionary definition of procrastination is "to put off doing something, especially out of habitual carelessness or laziness." The college definition procrastination is that you have five finals in the next two weeks, and you're reading this anyway.

Has anyone ever offered to split the reading with you before a final? That's a great idea - between the two of you, you'll get an A! Good thing the professor lets you take the exam in pairs.

Every semester, I keep a reverse tally of hours left until I'm done on my dry-erase board. I'd keep a tally of how many hours I study for each final, but I'm still trying to learn how to draw half a line.

You don't know real exhaustion until finals. I don't mind studying - but when you check e-mail forty times in one day, you're pretty wiped out.

It's not that seniors have fewer finals than everyone else, it's just that they don't care. By May, most seniors have jobs or have been accepted to grad school. And if they haven't, they're still smart enough to know that ten points on a calc final isn't going to help.

Reading week is the traditional period between the last day of classes and final exams that universities give students off to study. But at most schools, it's been shortened to one or two days. I guess Christmas had to get some of those twelve days from somewhere.

Why do some schools give their finals after break? A month after a class ends, I can't even tell you the name of my professor.

Professors are not supposed to give finals during reading week, but many of them do in order to end the semester early. That way, everyone can make their flight in time for the holidays, when they have to explain to their parents why they failed all of the finals given during reading week.

I came up with a formula to see how many finals someone has:
N = (days since shower + days since shave + times you used an academic reference to substitute for a punch line in the past week)/2

Studying for finals doesn't take that much time. It's taking the shrink-wrap off all my books that eats up my day.

When you have a ton of reading to do before finals, it's really frustrating. "600 pages by Monday? That's so unfair. They should have given us more time to do this. Like three months."

Why do some people leave school right after finals? The whole point of finals week is to work your ass off so that you can party when you're done. If you leave before you get a chance to party, that means you studied just for the sake of doing well. And what the hell good is that?

If you finish finals early, keep your mouth shut. You may think it's cool, but there is nothing other people hate more than the guy who finishes all his work first. Walk up to anyone and say, "I don't have finals and I kicked your baby brother in his stupid fat head." And they'll say, "What? You don't have finals?"

Ever look back at a midterm during finals and wish you could take it again? "How the hell did I get a C? I bet I'd get an A if I took it again today." Of course you would. Your midterm is just the first half of the test you're expected to ace tomorrow.

When you get to your last final of the semester, you are so burnt out that you don't even care. You studied half as much as you did for the other ones, you don't even remember to bring a pen, and when you finish, you don't check your answers over because you just want to hand it in and get the hell out of there. And you know why you can do that? Because you know that everyone else is doing the same thing.

CHAPTER 7

THE SUPPORTING CAST

You can have a wonderful time at the worst dive if you go there with the right people. And a place that should have the best ambience in the world could suck if populated with anyone that makes you uncomfortable. Likewise, your college experience is all about who you're surrounded with. Unfortunately, you don't get much choice in the matter.

There will be the colleagues that you can't choose – like the students in your classes, your clubs, and on the floor of your dorm. Then there are your superiors—the administration, professors, and resident advisors (I guess they're technically your superiors). And then the people that you have the least say in – people like the janitors, guards, and of course, your parents.

It's your parents that brought you here, and I don't just mean on move-in day. In most cases, they also pay for you to stay here, and that helps your relationship immensely. Because of your financial dependence, you still treat them well, and because of how bored they are without you, they treat you just as well. There's also that whole "becoming an adult thing," but I don't put much stock in it.

The janitors can become your friends because they clean up after you, which is a wonderful thing to someone whose parents are far away. But the guards are tough to deal with – because their job is to not let you in when you forget your ID.

You can choose what professors you have, to a point, but can get stuck with some bad ones if you need to take a certain class. And you're pretty much stuck with whatever advisor and RA they assign to you, which could either be a blessing or a curse. It's like playing poker. Sometimes, you draw a full house. Sometimes, you have a pair of twos. Most of the time, you'll probably have one or two royalty and the rest between a three and a seven.

But the college experience really comes down to the students. If you visit a school, you will almost always want to go there because you start thinking of the various ways you'd fit in. If you spend a weekend at a school and haven't thought about which dorm you'd live in and who you'd be friends with, run. Because enjoying college is all about the supporting cast.

High School Friends

There's always one guy who tries to set up reunions for your high school crew. Wonder how many college friends he has?

There are maybe three people from high school you still talk to, and it's only once a semester, yet you never seem to have anything to talk about. But when you go home for Thanksgiving, all you want to do is get back to school so you can see all of the friends you've missed for the past five days and catch up on everything you missed.

When you finally get together with the three high school friends you like, do you notice that all you do is reminisce? More cool stuff happened to you last week than in your entire high school experience, but all you can say when you see your old buddies is "man, remember that time junior year?"

Do you still remember what you got on your SATs? In high school, everyone knew what they got on all their tests, as well as the mean, median, and standard deviation of the entire grade. Now you can't even remember what you got on your midterm last week. If you can even remember taking a midterm last week.

Getting together with your high school friends is weird because you don't know who went to college and became a slut. And so you hit on everyone until you find her.

A five-year high school reunion could be fun, but it doesn't make much sense. "I haven't seen you in years! How have you been? Really? I just graduated, too! I don't have a family yet either! Oh my god, I'm also living on my own! I can't believe our lives have become so similar!"

You know what the quickest way to tell someone is a dork in college? If they keep reminding you of how cool they were in high school. If all their stories start out, "this one time in high school, man it was awesome" that's because nothing has been awesome for them since. A couple of key signs are a yearbook sitting open on the desk, a letter jacket on the very first hanger, and the constant desire to get back together with high school friends.

Parents

Thomas Holmes once wrote that you can never go home again. That's not true. You can go home, you just can't sleep in the same room as your girlfriend when you get there.

There are people who talk to their parents twice a day. They tell them everything about their classes, their roommates, even their hookups. Did you do this in high school? There's only so much stuff I can let my parents know about me before I start getting weirded out. That's why I went to school forty-five minutes from home. Far enough so they can't pop in all the time, but close enough so they don't feel they have to.

You really find out if you can get along with your parents if you can picture whether or not you could hang with them at school. Would your dad be one of those guys you know from a class or two that you pretend not to notice as you walk down the street and stare at the building just over his head, or the asshole from the football team that hits on all of your friends? Would your mom be the quiet mousy girl from the library who studies all day, or the slut who dances on the table *way* too early in the party? If you answered yes to any of these options, you do *not* get along with your parents.

It's weird when you go to your parents' house, because you've gotten so used to ultimate freedom. Your girlfriend or boyfriend comes over, and instead of hooking up all night before falling asleep in the same bed, you exchange sexually frustrated glances across the room and they sleep on your pullout in the living room. You can't drink, you can't smoke, and you don't have anyone paid to clean up after you. Why do you think everyone stops going home by sophomore year?

Packing your parents car with your dirty laundry because you don't want to do it yourself does not make you lazy. Taking three bags of laundry home on the bus, that's a different story.

Parents deal with your room in two ways once you leave for school. Either they rent it out for storage by the time you come back for Thanksgiving, or it remains a shrine to you for the next three decades. The first way, you can't go home. The second way, you don't want to.

Students

Not getting along with your roommate is understandable. But we all know one person who talks about how they don't get along with their roommate every single semester. Who do you think is the problem?

Some schools have you fill out a detailed questionnaire before they room you. They ask your likes, dislikes, ethnicity, habits, sleeping patterns, and shoe size. Then they enter all the data in a computer, use complicated procedures to find the closest mathematical matches, and pick your roommate's name out of a hat.

There's a guy in every class who never talks. When he's called on, he blankly says "uh," and slumps in his chair. He speaks once at the end of the semester and the teacher bumps his grade up a point for improving. Which is nice, because then he can keep his athletic scholarship.

You know that one girl who always asks the dumb questions? Does she notice that the entire class groans when she puts her hand up? How can she miss the fact that eighty people are making fun of her? Probably because she sits in the front row, and can't see any of them.

Some people go to classes strictly because they want to get the most for their money. What is this, a salad bar? I want good grades because I want a good job because I want to send my kid to school so they can do the same for theirs. If that means going to class, then so be it. Otherwise, I'm staying home and getting some sleep - I pay to be able to do that too.

I'd love to see one more section on a roommate compatibility questionnaire: "Do you plan to have a permanent girlfriend or boyfriend? And if so, will they be living with you, or will you be living with them?"

Some roommates' parents tell you too much. So you end up taking a message that says, "his grandmother came out of the operation fine, the divorce papers went through, and that the doctor says it's not leprosy—but the herpes tests haven't come back yet." Thanks. I can sleep much easier now.

Professors

Some professors do not give As, so you ask them why. "I'm sorry," they say, "I don't give As." Hey, buddy, it's your job to give 'A's sometimes. If you don't think anyone you've ever taught deserves an A, then maybe they're not the ones who need improvement.

I've discovered the secret to doing well in class. Stay quiet the first two or three weeks. Then approach the teacher after a class and tell them how you're really trying, and you want to do well in the specific subject because your brother/cousin/dog is really good at it and you're trying so hard to have them approve of you and then ask what the professor thinks you should do. Whatever they suggest, don't actually do it. But during the next class, raise your hand like thirty times. Your ego driven professor will be so impressed with themselves for helping you that they'll up your grade a full point.

Some professors are funny. All professors *think* they are funny.

Every professor thinks their class is the most important one you have. I can understand that for the professors teaching any kind of advanced class. But when it's midterm week and you teach the "Welcome to College" seminar, you can pretty much figure that no one is going to complete your assignment to make a map of the campus library.

Why are there some psychology professors that are shut-ins? If I claimed to understand human nature, I'd know the best way to get a raise, have a date every night, and be able to make anyone laugh or cry with a few choice words. Having a tool for a psych professor is like having a health teacher that smokes.

Teachers can get personally offended if you don't know the material they assigned. But even weirder is when they expect you to know random stuff from classes you've never taken. I had a history professor who would always reference the most advanced stuff that we never learned in class, and act like it was common knowledge. What he forgot was that he devoted his entire life to learning about the Louisiana Purchase, and the closest we've ever come to it is that one Spring Break at Mardi Gras.

Administrators

There's got to be someone, somewhere, with enough of a sense of humor to write their name on their office door in red tape.

I think every university president should have to eat in the dining hall once a month. Not so that he can see what's really going on in the school, or so that students will have a chance to interact with him, but so he can taste what they're feeding us.

You can tell if you go to a school with a male-dominated board of trustees by who the deans are. If the deans are guys, you do not go to a male-dominated school. If the deans are hot women in their twenties, figure it out.

Why don't presidents just cut to the chase and call themselves CEOs?

I love the administrators that do absolutely nothing; their only job is to send you to other people. I bet if you ask them point blank for their job requirements, they'll tell you that they're the "dean of, um, stuff."

Deans

In high school, you had a principal and an assistant principal to kiss up to. In college, you have 473 deans. Better get some chapstick.

How great would it be to work as an office assistant in a college and just happen to be named Dean?

There's a dean for everything at my school. Dean of Students. Dean of Student Affairs. Assistant Dean of Student Affairs. Assistant Dean of Student Affairs and Special Programming. The title "Dean" is kind of like "Associate Producer."

Would the Dean of Food Services get pissed if you call him Jimmy?

We have something called "Dean's Discipline" at my school. That's when you do something wrong and you are at the complete mercy of a dean when it comes to punishment, which some people think is unfair. But how are we going to learn to use fascism later in life if they don't teach it to us now?

Alumni

I'm going to help my school raise money when I graduate, but I'm not going to do it by giving them any. I figure that if they don't constantly send me letters asking for donations, they'll save a few bucks on stamps.

I don't understand the concept of admitting legacies into schools, clubs, or teams. If smart, cool, and athletic were dominant genes, don't you think we'd know by now? Sure, some of them are coincidentally very skilled. But the only thing that's hereditary about them is money.

What's with alumni who come to all of the football games? Some are a few years out of school and want to see people they know. Some are older men and women who want to find something to do on a Saturday. But the guys who have been at every single game for the last twenty years? We're horrible at football. But our team is adept at attracting fans who appreciate a good three-touchdown loss.

Why don't adults remember college? Most people's parents have no idea what goes on at school, even though its been going on since colleges existed. Apparently the last class you take is brainwashing. If you get anything above a three on the final, you have to take it again.

Only alumni with uncommon names donate money to my school. Our buildings are named Schermerhorn, Sulzberger, and Fayerweather. What the hell happened to Smith?

Why does it matter so much to people what school you went to? Every time I meet a Columbia alum, they get all excited about it. Except when people my parents' age went to Columbia, we were the nation's focus due to a protest for social justice. Now, we're very proud of our football team's three-win season.

Everyone knows the Freshman 15. Less publicized is the Alumni 18.

The first few months of senior year, all you want to do is graduate. But the first few months working, all you want to do is go back. It's not that the grass is always greener, it's just that the first few months of senior year and the first few months of working both suck pretty hard.

Bouncers

I once heard someone ask at what point someone becomes a bouncer. I'm pretty sure it's about two weeks after they get cut from the team.

It must be weird to be a regular bouncer at a college bar. When you're at work, you're a total god. Everyone wants to be your friend. You have girls constantly coming up and hugging and kissing you, and you get tons of free alcohol. But what happens when it's all over? I knew a guy who went from being a bouncer to a doorman at a fancy apartment building. Suddenly, he gets in trouble for not recognizing people, has to let everyone in, and instead of getting a raise for beating someone up, he gets fired.

Bouncers, to bar goers, are your well-being. They allow you to enter that mystical bar world that people always feel they need to enter for social success. But for some reason, people argue with them. When you meet a new bouncer, convince them how you were friends with the old one and make sure to shake their hand every time you leave. That's the only way to sneak in your friend that looks like he's twelve.

I hate the bouncers that try to show power by carding extra hard. Its one thing to do your job, its another to be a prick. They quiz you on your birthday and address before they let you pay their salary. Guess what? If no one gets into the bar, they don't work anymore and become something like bus drivers. Then how do you ID people? "I'm sorry sir, I can't let you on. You and I both know that's not your real bus fare."

There's one bar near me that had a problem with the cops, so it asks you for your ID and your school ID. Which would be fine, except the bouncer doesn't really understand that some of the people who go to bars aren't in school. I once watched him spend ten minutes rejecting a thirty-two year old guy cause he didn't have an ID that said he was underage like the rest of us.

My favorite kind of bouncer is the little guy. The guy that never works his own shift because if he tried to stop any trouble, he'd get his ass kicked. Ever wonder what happened to the short little friend of the grade school bully? Stop wondering.

Guards

A guard yelled at me because I was blocking the path between the staircase and the elevator. Because so many people take stairs to get to the elevator.

Guards at college have three main jobs - one is to sign people in to a dorm and another is to drive people home when they have too much to drink. Apparently, their third job is too watch soap operas on a TV with bad reception. Talking on the phone and ignoring you when you're trying to speak to them isn't in their job description, but most of them are studying to be receptionists at my doctor's office.

Campus security isn't such a protecting force. They don't have guns, they don't have billy clubs, and they're not even allowed to arrest you. But nothing deters a crime like a guy in a funny hat saying, "hey, quit it."

One guard didn't let me into my friend's dorm because it was spring, and the last validation I had on my ID was from the fall. She insisted that I give her current proof of ID. I said, "I think you're a moron, and if I think, therefore I am." She didn't appreciate the philosophy behind it.

I was once pretty loud with a friend of mine on the steps of our library, and campus security came over and told us to settle down. What are they going to do, threaten to drive us home?

Janitors

Cleaning up after college kids is the worst job in the world. When a janitor cleans a lounge full of beer bottles, pizza boxes, and vomit, he must be thinking "damn these kids had fun last night." Then he thinks "I'm cleaning broken glass, stale cheese, and someone else's puke."

Janitors have shirts with their names sewn on? Mechanics and gas station attendants have this too. Why are those professions where you need to know someone's first name? When faced with a janitor or a lawyer, who would you rather call, "Hey buddy"?

I was never one of those people who knew all the maintenance staff's names. At what point do you say, "I know you're busy cleaning my friend's vomit, but we've never been properly introduced. I'm Steve."

Resident Advisors

Some RAs are awesome. Others make door decorations with your name written on the silhouette of a farm animal.

"Freshman RA" is not short for "Freshman Resident Advisor." It's short for "Freshman Resident Advisor That Spends Two Days Making Cut-Outs With Everyone's Name and Room On Them, Only To Watch the Freshmen Rip Them Down the First Week." Thought I'd clear that up.

Sophomore year, my RA was a guy I'd known since I was twelve. I ran in to him in the bathroom one night, my eyes watery, my clothes smelling like smoke, and my breath reeking of alcohol - and he was totally cool with it. Looking back, I think it was less because we were friends and more because he had already been puking for the last three hours.

I know one guy who used to take condoms from our RA every day just to make people think he was having sex. When he moved out of his room, his closet looked like that kid's locker in the Pop Tarts commercial.

Busting your residents when they're passed out drunk is like telling a professor that the kid next to you has fallen asleep in class. Just nudge the guy with your shoulder until he wakes up - in both scenarios.

There's this whole application process to determine who gets to be an RA. And though some RAs are awesome, for some reason, they still accept a few total freaks. I think it's just so all the decent kids in those halls will see how bad their RAs are and decide to become one just so they can be better than the guy they had.

I respect authority. But an RA's only recourse is to call other people to tell them something is wrong. That is less authority, and more being someone's kiss-up little brother.

If you think about it, schools set RAs up for failure. An RA is supposed to keep the floor substance free *and* give thoughtful guidance at the same time. "I'm three weeks late for my period and I really need some advice. I know - I'll go talk to the chick who spilled out my beer and turned me in for smoking pot. I feel like she really understands me."

I Killed My RA Today
Another Student Body Shots Song

Again, the chords here are simple - Gs, Cs, and Ds, and Ems. And again, if your cover band can come up with a better progression or a good version of this one, record the mp3 and send it to collegehumor@yahoo.com.

```
G                    Em
I went to some old campus bar
C                          D
Got hammered with some friends
G                    Em
I thought the night went pretty well
C              G
Until it neared its end.
```
The speed I used to down my beer
Seemed almost past unreal
So I went to use the bathroom
Cause I had to break my seal

I killed my RA today
Oh why'd he have to go away
The birds are dead, the sky is gray
The whole world just plain sucks
They'll question me and I'll say no
I'll run away and just lay low
I need to find a place to go
Or I'll get written up

As I approached the men's room
I spotted my RA
He shouldn't see me drinking
So I tried to walk away.
I tried to go unnoticed
But I bumped into a chair
The whole bar turned to look at me
And my RA saw me there

I knew I was in trouble
And I knew that it was plenty
He's allowed to drink but I am not
Even though he's only twenty
A wave of dread swept over me
Followed close by drunken fear
So I did the only thing I could
And brained him with my beer.

I killed my RA today
Oh why'd he have to go away
The birds are dead, the sky is gray
The whole world just plain sucks
They'll question me and I'll say no
I'll run away and just lay low
I need to find a place to go
Or I'll get written up

I spilled and hit him way too hard
Cause he flew from his chair
And fell into a cigarette
As flame engulfed his hair
He stopped, dropped, rolled to put it out
But then he hit his head
And lay there just becoming bald
Or that's what his boyfriend said.

I killed my RA today
Oh why'd he have to go away
The birds are dead, the sky is gray
The whole world just plain sucks
They'll question me and I'll say no
I'll run away and just lay low
I need to find a place to go
Or I'll get written up

CHAPTER 8

FACILITIES

It's amazing what humans can adapt to. If you and a roommate live in a ten-by-ten box your freshman year, you will be thrilled to have an eight-by-eight room to yourself the following year. But for some inexplicable reason, colleges never make all housing equal. Every year, there are some freshmen with shacks and some with suites, some sophomores with hovels and some with homes, and some juniors with manholes and some with mansions. Seniors always get good housing.

The facilities that colleges use are always quirky, because schools tend to cut corners whenever possible. There are classrooms that have projectors that slide down from the ceiling, while others force their professors to use a crude system of bed sheets and smoke signals. Some dorms are wired for Ethernet, while others at the same university have you connecting through AOL. And some buildings on campus are decrepit and falling apart, while others are the president's house.

I already started telling you about the library as a social scene, but I'll get deeper into that building with all the books. And there are plenty of other places that are standards on college campi—like communal bathrooms, the gym, and dining halls. Dining halls are perhaps the best standards eliminator that college campi have. We buy undercooked food at overinflated prices, and don't really mind because it's our only choice at schools where you have to be on the meal plan. And then, when we take more of the horrible food than we should, we brag to each other about how we snuck off with free grub.

Bathrooms decrease our standards almost as much. Though we grew up with the privacy of single bathrooms, we now all shower together, and most times, men do so without shower stalls. We also have to relieve ourselves in groups, and we can't leave our shampoo or anything else in the bathroom, lest it get stolen within minutes of our putting it there. College bathrooms are a cross between those at the Y and a football game, but a little less private and slightly dirtier.

And we don't really complain. Actually, we complain all the time, but we don't really mean it - and we never think of actually doing anything about it. Whatever doesn't kill you makes you stronger, so we must have real ultimate power by now. After all, we've survived the facilities.

Dorms

Colleges are very good at distributing floors equally. No matter how many rooms there are and how many people per room, there is exactly one person on every floor who listens to crappy music way too loud.

Why does no one care how thin the walls are? A bed creek, unavoidable. The occasional thumping of a flailing arm into a wall, acceptable. But moaning at 4:00 in the afternoon? No sex can be that good that you can't shut up, bite down on a blanket and let me study.

How ineffective are the dorm rules they gave us during orientation? I figured out that halogen lamps must work well in dorm rooms because of that little flier that tells us not to use them. How many of us even knew what a halogen lamp was before we read that?

Dorm rooms prepare you to live anywhere and be happy. You spend four years living in an eight-by-eight room, and you get to the real world and have to find an apartment. The first one you see is a studio, and all you can think is "this is the biggest single I have seen in my entire life."

Why does every school have at least one really crappy dorm? And every dorm has at least one really crappy room? Hey college - stop building crappy rooms, okay? Thanks - we appreciate it.

People get so excited by their friends' housing lottery numbers. "My friend got number 2,998 out of 3000! Isn't that wild?" "No way, dude, my friend was number twenty-three!" "Woah - my friend was, like, seventeen!" Hey - no one really cares what your friends' lottery numbers are. Besides, I had a friend who was number four. Isn't that wild?

There's constantly signs advertising on my campus for people to help fill the last few spaces in suites. I think it would be smarter to post signs looking for a roommate who is going abroad the whole year. Or at least someone with a girlfriend across town.

If I got number one in the housing lottery, I'd sell it to number fifty for $100, sell that to number 100, sell that to 200, and so on. I'd end up with the worst room on campus, but it'd be wallpapered in solid gold.

Bathrooms

Bathrooms are scary. Not because we don't know where things there have been. It's cause we know exactly where things there have been.

There are two types of all male bathrooms. The first type has toilet paper all over the place, water dripping from the side of the sink, and porno magazines strewn all over the floor. The second type has toilet paper all over the place, water dripping from the side of the sink, and a neat little stack of porno magazines in the corner.

Some guys say that the reason why they piss on the seat is because it was dark and they couldn't find the light. Ever thought of sitting down?

It's rough to be the only male in the hallway of an all girls dorm when someone discovers piss on the seat. Even if you haven't gone to that bathroom in two weeks it's your fault just for being anatomically able.

I accepted girls going to the bathroom together a long time ago, but not when it happens in a suite with a one-person bathroom. I don't care what is going on in there. I just want to know how they fit.

Guys use the bathroom quicker than girls. It has nothing to do with anatomy – it's just that talking is discouraged.

I don't understand why no one else on my floor knows how to plunge a toilet. It's a pretty simple skill – you put the plunger in, you press down on it, and you take it out. These are the same people who know every last Smash Brothers move but they don't know how to stop crap from flowing all over the floor. Good thing they learned what's important.

Male bathrooms are smaller than female bathrooms. Not only do urinals take up less space than stalls, but men can't figure out what to do with eight square feet of counter space.

In girls' dorms, there are girls' bathrooms and "co-ed" bathrooms. But the girls only use the girls' bathroom since the two are right next to each other. Schools need to suck it up and call the co-ed bathroom the men's room. Yes, guys stay over in the dorm. And yes, they pee, too.

Dining Halls

The campus dining hall. Where the leaders of tomorrow eat the leftovers of yesterday.

I had a friend who decided that because the dining hall was all you can eat, he'd get his money's worth. So my friend packed on two-dozen extra pounds freshman year from stuffing his face with moderate tasting food every night until he was sick. I don't think he won that battle.

My school added a stir-fry bar to one of the dining halls. Which is great for everyone bored of eating stuff cooked by professionals. Now we can pay an extra dollar and screw up the meal ourselves.

Schools charge your parents thirteen bucks a meal for crappy pizza and a whole bunch of vegan food when you could be spending four dollars on lo-mein and a coke. And everyone always has fifty meals left in the last week of the semester. Schools don't prohibit hotplates for safety, they do it so you're forced to eat in the dining hall instead of spending twelve cents on a bowl of Top Ramen.

I told my friend that dating someone who worked in our dining hall was sketchy. She got mad at me and criticized me for treating him like he's some untouchable peon only meant to prepare food for us. Actually, I thought it was sketchy because he was forty years old with a wife and two kids, but why quibble over semantics?

One of my dining halls was divided up in the worst way. If you wanted a sandwich, you had to wait on line to order it. Then, you had to wait on line to pick it up. Then, you had to wait on line to pay for it. Then, it tasted like ass. And you had to wait on line to throw it out.

On most meal plans, you get guest meals. But you only get like three per semester. I thought that was a ridiculously small amount of times you could bring a friend to dinner. Then I remembered that after freshman year, no one is friends with anyone outside of school anyway.

I know stealing dining hall silverware is wrong, but at thirteen bucks a meal, you should get to keep the fork.

Libraries

Colleges have huge libraries with hundreds of thousands of books, so they need a complex system of numbers and maps to tell you exactly which shelf your book was supposed to be on before it was misplaced.

College libraries should not be social scenes. In the real world, you meet someone at a library because people there are well read. In college, people are in the library because they don't get along with their roommates enough to study in their own rooms.

I know someone who won't go to the stacks because he's afraid of people hooking up. But he'll still go to the bathroom at a bar and into his dorm's lounge without thinking twice.

College students brag about how rarely they go to the library.
"I've only been to the library twice this semester."
"Oh yeah? I've only been to the library once since I've been at school."
"Yeah? I don't even know where the library is."
"Oh man, that's awesome."
Rough translation:
"I'm not that bright."
"Oh yeah? I'm even dumber."
"Yeah? I'm an utter moron, and very proud of my limited intelligence."
"Oh man, that's awesome."

I saw someone kick someone else out of a library study carrel because it was "his." I'm not talking about someone who was there first, and called fives. I'm talking a turf war where a guy claimed a section of the room. What he doesn't realize is even if he wins, he's already lost.

The library is a great place to study. By the time I leave, I haven't looked at my reading, but I am the world's foremost expert on seventeen different people's pen fidgets, snacking habits, and bathroom intervals.

College library books are never where they're supposed to be. See, guys like me make seven dollars an hour to shelve them, and until that changes, fast food will never be what you ordered, packages will never arrive on time, and books will never be in the right place. Ever.

The Gym

When you work out for the first time in a while, you have a lot to do when you get back. You have to shower, you have to change, and you have to tell everyone you run into that you just back from the gym.

You're not healthy just because you work out. You eat Ramen for lunch, pizza for dinner, and you've never been awake for breakfast. You drink all weekend, spend your free time IMing your roommate, and have to smoke a cigarette in order to go to sleep - at 4:00 AM on a Tuesday. But those three sets of bicep curls? Man, they're keeping you healthy.

If I had a gym in my own place, I would work out every day. But I can't even fit a chair in my own place, so that's sort of out of the question.

Every time I go to the gym, I want to take off my glasses because I don't like to wear them while I work out. But I don't do it because not being able to see well defeats the real purpose of going to the gym.

The first time I ever went to the gym, I asked my friend where the bathroom was. He hushed me and said I should be quieter or everyone will know that I didn't go to the gym so often. Yeah, that bathroom comment was the only thing that gave it away.

T-shirts with the sleeves cut off don't help you lift better. "Those sleeves really constricted my arms. Now that I'm showing off my muscle, I can bench twice as much!"

It's hard to motivate yourself to go to the gym. I may love the feeling I get when I finish a workout, but I love the feeling I get when I finish a paper, and it doesn't make me write one every day.

I try to impress girls with how much I can lift. So whenever a cute one walks by, I artificially inflate the number of reps I have actually done. "Seven! Arrrr...eight! Niiiiiine!"

I do pushups every night at the beginning of every year, but I usually stop a month or two later. It's not because I am lazy or week willed. It's because I get increasingly frightened of what's been on the floor.

CHAPTER 9

HOLIDAYS AND EVENTS

"Michelob makes every occasion seem special."
-That commercial with the guys lifting their arms funny

While it's done with something even cheaper than Michelob, college kids find any reason to party. We throw parties for Valentine's Day, the day before Thanksgiving, welcome back to school, Tuesday; if it has happened, a college student has probably thrown a party in its honor. And though sometimes parties are thrown for no particular reason at all, most college parties are themed, and thus college students take whatever excuse they can to celebrate some holiday ritual. Or rather create their own ritual that just coincides with some kind of holiday.

The most common of the college holiday parties are probably the Halloween party, the Winter Holiday party, and the end of the year blow out. The Halloween party usually involves beer and candy, which can be a dangerous combination. The Winter Holiday party usually involves beer and mistletoe, which can be even more dangerous. And the end of the year blowout usually involves beer and no responsibility at all, which can be the most dangerous thing of all.

People throw birthday parties, New Year's parties, Super Bowl parties, Cinquo de Mayo parties, State of the Union parties, and parties for any other reason they can think of. People like to throw parties not because they enjoy going to them, but because they enjoy having been the one to get credit for everyone else having such a good time.

But there's more to these holidays and events than just parties. There are the vacations, where no one is around to come to your party if you throw one. Like Thanksgiving, where the idea is to have a big dinner with your entire family and everyone they've ever met. Or winter break, where you sit in your room, lamenting your lack of Ethernet and play. Or summer break, where you get a job and become increasingly frightened of the post-college world. If it weren't for spring break, vacations wouldn't be fun. Well, if it weren't for the parts of spring break that we can remember.

Holidays and special events are able to drag us out of our routines, if just for a day. That is what makes them holy and/or special.

Birthdays

What do you get for the student that has everything? More beer.

No matter where you go on your twenty-first, you will not be carded. Unless you forget your ID. Then you'll be carded everywhere. Twice.

I feel bad for the people that turn twenty-one in January. Sure, *they* don't have to worry about getting into bars anymore. And if there's one fun way to go to a bar, it's by yourself.

The month before you turn twenty-one will be the most awkward month of your entire life. You don't want to lie and say that you're already twenty-one, but you know if you say you're twenty, you'll feel cheated. I constantly found myself telling people I was in my early twenties, because technically I was. Yeah, and Rhode Island is also technically a state, but you don't find it bragging much.

Someone once yelled at me to shut my music off, and said I had to listen to them because it was their birthday. Which was helpful, since I knew how old they were before I turned my music up and laughed.

Why do we still write people's names on the envelope of their birthday card? I guess it avoids confusion when roommates have the same birthday, since that happens all the time.

Twenty-two is such a let-down birthday. Now I know how 2001 felt.

If 40 is over the hill, then 22 is the first time you set up base camp.

Weekday birthdays are not bad because you can't go out - they're bad because you have classes. Nothing says "happy birthday" like 300 pages of reading and a two-hour lecture.

In college, everyone combines birthdays. There are really only three days a week that people can party, so everyone with a birthday within a few days of a particular weekend decides to celebrate together on a particular night. I can never remember my friends' birthdays because every year they're different.

Halloween

Before you hook up with someone at a Halloween party, make sure it's actually a mask.

Every college Halloween party has at least one guest who is too lazy to dress up. So they'll say they're wearing a costume, using the same joke that the rest of us used in eighth grade. "You're going as a stressed out student, and really you're just wearing your every day clothing, as if to say that you're stressed out all the time? Oh, how galatically clever!"

When you were younger, you'd go trick or treating for what you'd really want--candy. In college, all any of us ever really want is play. Wouldn't it be awesome if we could still go trick or treating? Like when you were a kid, you'll get a few people who will slam the door on you, and a few who will give you something you don't want, like fruit or some pennies. But in any given year, if you went through the whole neighborhood and got just one really good candy bar, wasn't it worth it?

Since you can't when you're younger, some kids buy a ton of candy freshman year just because they can. If you think a hangover is bad, try waking up the day after you finish a three-pound bag of candy corn.

One Halloween I wore cat ears, angel wings, and carried a pitch fork, and went as every freaking girl on my campus.

When Halloween falls on a Saturday, you party for three days. When if falls on a Monday, you party for five. When it falls on a Wednesday, that's seven days of partying. But something definitely feels weird about a Halloween party on October 25th. Maybe because you can't get away with smacking someone in the back of the head during the last week of March and telling them that it's April Fool's Day weekend.

Have you ever looked at someone's costume and thought, "Wow, that's creative?" What you should be saying is "why do you own that?"

I know a girl who spent $100 on the perfect Halloween costume that she wore for three hours. But she can't spend the extra fifty cents to avoid drinking Natty Lite.

Election Day

A political candidate is like the junk you fill your dorm room with freshman year. Yeah, it makes sense now, but in four years, you're going to look back and wonder why you bought any of it.

All of our presidents went to college. And they made some mistakes their first year, just like the rest of us. By the second or third year, they got the hang of things, but in the fourth, they realized it'll all be over soon and they'll need a job. So they either found one or decided to stay where they were another few years. College was also tough.

Either the drinking age needs to be lowered to eighteen or the voting age needs to be upped to twenty-one. After choosing between the candidates we usually have, the country needs a good strong drink.

In the last presidential election, I chose Gore over Bush. Though when it comes to renting movies, I'm usually the other way around.

Bush publicized his involvement in DKE to try and get the college vote. Think of your friend who always stumbles into his room at 5:00 AM, throws up on the floor, sleeps in it, and then asks you why he's so tired the next day. Now imagine everyone calling him Mr. President.

When a political candidate comes to my campus, I don't want him to tell me how "hip" or "cool" he is, and how he can "get down with" my problems if I am willing to "rap" with him. I want him to admit he's an out of touch old guy that hasn't been in college in forty years, but he'll still be willing to bomb the hell out of anyone that messes with us.

We can register for classes, bid on Ferraris, and make long-distance calls on the web, but the only way to vote is in a giant punch block-based booth with a huge red lever. When it was my turn, I wasn't sure if I needed a number two pencil or a pair of ruby slippers.

Every election, there are like eight candidates I've never even heard of. These are the same guys that ran and lost for student council four years in a row. Face it man - no matter how many posters you put up, you just won't win. Save the world some masking tape and go home.

Thanksgiving

Thanksgiving is the best holiday to find out who is rich and who isn't. The rich people fly across the country for two days, while the poor people try to find their closest friend who lives in the area.

Campus is so empty the night before Thanksgiving that it feels like you're in Independence Day, combing the bars for survivors. "I thought they had cleared this area already, but it's good to find some others. You look woozy - we'll get something to take care of that. I know you called this place home, but things are different. We're all rendezvousing in a few hours. Sir, let it go – it's time to move on to the next bar."

Every year, it seems that Thanksgiving gets longer and longer. Freshman year, most people went home Wednesday night. Sophomore year, people didn't want to deal with flying in late and started booking flights for Wednesday morning. By junior year, people went home the weekend before. If I ever go to grad school, I think I'm going to see the first forty-seven-day weekend in history.

In any given week, you pray that somehow, someway, you can just get two extra hours to finish your work in time. So you get a four-day weekend right before finals, and how do you spend it? Watching Sylvestor Stallone and Clint Eastwood marathons on TBS and eating leftovers from Thursday night. Then you get back to school, realize you have a paper due that week, and pray that somehow, someway, you can just get two extra hours to finish your work in time.

When I was a kid, I remember waking up first thing Thanksgiving morning to watch the parade. What the hell was I thinking? I guess the balloons can keep a kid entertained, but the high school bands and B-list celebrities singing songs I've never head of are just not worth setting my alarm for. Then again, neither is a 9:00 class.

It makes perfect sense that turkey and wine both make you tired. The typical Thanksgiving dinner involves your siblings quizzing you on who you've ever dated, your mom asking you what your GPA *really* is, and all your extended family discussing their insurance policies and recent operations. The earlier I get to sleep, the happier I am.

Christmas & Hannukah

Whoever invented mistletoe is a genius. But whoever limited its use to one month each year is a cruel bastard.

I hate how over-hyped and commercialized Hannukah has gotten. As soon as they stroll that giant menorah down Fifth Avenue to end the Thanksgiving Day parade, I'm like, "crap, another month of dreidels." If I hear one more Hannukah song on the radio, I'm going to lose it.

Not everyone celebrates Christmas. I mentioned to someone that I was staying at school over break, and they asked if I got along with my family so poorly that we couldn't even put aside our differences on the holiest of Christian holidays. "Yeah," I said. "It's pretty rough - apparently, my parents just won't forgive me for being born Jewish."

I don't freak out when someone wishes me a Merry Christmas, even though I'm Jewish. I want to be merry on December 25th just like every one else. I just won't be doing it in front of a tree.

The older I get, the more I have to spend on presents. I used to glue some macaroni on a card and my parents would say it's the best present they ever got. Now if it doesn't come with a receipt, no one wants it.

When Adam Sandler first wrote that Hannukah song, I thought it was great to finally have a holiday song for my religion. And then I realized that our songs played 300 times a day are just as annoying.

Every TV show has a Christmas special - even ones with Jewish characters. But South Park is the one that deals with Hannukah. Seinfeld has an episode about Christmas cards, and the only representation that Jews get is from an eight-year-old cartoon character that plays with a turd in a little red hat. And they say Jews control Hollywood.

Some campuses are incorrectly politically correct when it comes to the winter holidays. The traditional "Merry Christmas" is now followed by "Happy Hanukkah" and "Happy Kwaanza." But some people say "Happy Ramadan." Do they have any idea how solemn Ramadan is? That's like wishing an Organic Chemistry major a "Happy Finals Week."

Winter Break

When you go home for winter break, you're like "Score! A month off!" Then you spend a week with no drinking, lots of nagging, and the terrible thought that you have three more weeks of this.

Some parents plan a dinner or snacks or something when you get back for the holidays and say it's for you but invite all of their friends and none of yours. Then you're surrounded by people you hardly know who are all pretending to be extremely interested in your major and telling you how much growing you've done while they talk to each other about their insurance plans. Weeeeeee.

When you leave for break, you should plan on getting to an airport an hour or two before your flight, but plan on leaving three more hours before that. Because the last night before you go home, you are never in the condition to methodically pack everything you own. Or wake up.

I worked the first two weeks of a break, but had absolutely nothing to do for the next two weeks. I planned on using the time to write, fix up my resume, and go to the gym. Actually, I just sat on my couch and watched SportsCenter, but everyone needs goals.

Why do they have to give us a whole month at once? I'd make December break be two weeks. Give me an extra two days to study for finals, an actual day off in the middle of April, and an extra long weekend every two weeks for the entire spring semester, and we'll call it even.

So there's this holiday where everyone is supposed to get a kiss at midnight - except it happens in the one month of the year that we're living with our parents. Thanks, God. That was a good one.

New Year's resolutions were cute when we were in fourth grade. But in college, we make and break them every week. "Next time I'll do the reading." "That's the last time I get with someone from my floor." "I'll never drink again." Why set ourselves up for failure? Last year, my resolutions were to live in my fraternity house, buy Cliffs Notes for every book, and go out any time my friends wanted to - and dammit, I feel like I'm a better person for accomplishing all three.

Valentine's Day

It's sad to see the bar scene on Valentine's Day. Especially on a Monday.

Valentine's Day in college is a little easier than it was in when we were in high school. In both cases, no one wants to be alone. But this time everyone has alcohol.

Valentine's Day at school is weird. All the couples make out in the middle of campus, all the single girls write poetry about how bad Valentine's Day is, and all the single guys try to get the single girls drunk so they'll stop writing poetry and hook up with them.

Have you ever gotten one of these on-line crush things? You get a chance to list everyone you have a crush on, and then they all get an e-mail telling them that someone likes them. So they get an opportunity to list you back - or anyone else for that matter. If you list each other, then you both instantly find out and are able to begin your otherwise lost love affair. But half the time that you list anyone, it winds up being someone you don't like at all just to see if they're the one who sent it to you in the first place.

You can't break up with someone right before their birthday, formal, or Valentine's Day. So if your girl has a spring birthday, no matter when you figure out you're unhappy, you have to date her right up until June.

The symbol of Valentine's Day is a baby who shoots people, you're pressured to give a girl chocolate and watch her complain about how insensitive you are because she's on a diet, and fourth graders decide who is cool and who is not by their amounts of pieces of paper with poorly cut ribbon and too much glitter. But it's sweet, really.

It'd be fun to go to a florist the day after Valentine's Day and figure out how much a guy screwed up by how many flowers he is buying.

Valentine's Day and the last night of school are the two easiest nights for a guy to hook up. See, for 365 nights a year, guys are looking to get some. But Valentine's Day and the last night of school are the only days that most girls are, too.

Passover

Passover is simple to explain. It's Thanksgiving without bread or football.

A friend of mine asked me if I had a happy Passover, without realizing it was still going on. Passover is eight days. Hannukah is eight days. Sukkot is eight days. See, we buy everything wholesale.

I prefer Passover to Thanksgiving. At Thanksgiving, some of your relatives will drone on and on for hours about what they have to be thankful for, and why they're all so blessed to have made it another year. That happens at Passover too, but at least there's a script.

It's a Passover tradition to serve both egg soup and chicken soup. Though for the life of me, I can't remember which comes first.

The ten plagues were blood, frogs, vermin, pestilence, cattle death, boils, hail, locusts, darkness, and the slaying of the first born. If it weren't for that last one, I'd think I was praying to El Nino.

Easter

I used to think that Easter Island was a whole island filled with chocolate and bunnies, but it turns out that it's just a bunch of mean looking stone faces. Which makes sense, since that's how a lot of my friends describe hanging out with their relatives.

Good Friday is supposed to be a fast day. Except I found out you get one main meal, and then another small meal to keep you going. That's not fasting - that's Jenny Craig.

It's funny when people give up things they don't enjoy doing for lent, in an effort to trick God. I like to think of God as someone who can't be fooled into thinking that I'm struggling to end my addiction to homework.

I know an overweight, chain-smoking alcoholic who couldn't come up with anything to give up for lent. She settled on "three years of her life."

Painted eggs, wicker baskets, chocolate, and marshmallows molded in the shape of bunnies and baby chicks? The only rebirth Easter commemorates is that of Martha Stewart's career.

Summer Vacation

When you have a week off in March, you go to Cancun. When you have all of June, July, and August, you go to work. Makes perfect sense.

People with summer jobs don't go out on weekdays so they can get some sleep. It's important to be wide-awake while you sit there instant messaging other people who didn't go out the night before.

I never took a summer class. Do you know that first day when the weather starts getting really nice, and everybody hangs out outside because its just impossible to go to class? Make that class three hours a day for four days a week, raise the temperature about ten degrees, have that day last two entire months, and then see how you feel.

When you're not doing much, having lunch is an excellent way to break up the day. You know, between not having lunch and not having lunch.

Being at home is tough. Your laundry is done for you, your meals are home cooked, and you never have homework. But trying to download MP3s without ethernet, man that's a pain in the ass.

If you stay at school, you collect your supporting cast for the summer the first few days of break. "Um, I'll take my best friend, the guy from my freshman floor, that girl from my history class, and some dude I met when I went to get some pizza."

I know some people who took a low paying summer job with bad hours because it's in the field that they want to pursue. Photocopying.

Most summer jobs are excellent networking opportunities. And I don't mean for your career - I mean for your social life. At any big company, there are usually a dozen other kids your age, most of whom have reasonably attractive friends that you have yet to alienate.

Summer jobs are not as tough as a few months working in the real world. Unless it's in finance. Then it's as tough as a few *years* working in the real world. I know people with jobs in finance this summer. Actually, I *knew* people with jobs in finance. I'll know them again in September.

Other Holidays

What professors assign work over Spring Break? Don't they understand that it's tough to do the reading during a keg stand?

Who decides where spring break is every year? One year it was Cancun, one year it was Miami Beach, one year it was St. Thomas. I would love to be the one to decide, so I could be like, "yeah, this year it's Cleveland."

You know that "Too Hot For TV" with all the footage of girls stripping during spring break? Their angle is that these are prototypical college girls out on break, and so they advertise it as "the girls next door." I remember the girls who lived next door my freshman year. And I can assure you that no one would pay $9.95 to see them naked.

What happened to all the little holidays we used to get in high school? Election Day? Veterans Day? Presidents Day? Are these not holidays anymore? In college, Abraham Lincoln is still a great guy, but not quite cool enough to get a three-day weekend.

The timing for Cinquo de Mayo couldn't be worse. Here it is, a holiday where people celebrate with nachos and Corona but everyone is stuck in the library. Not me - I think studying instead of nachos and Corona is like vacuuming during the Super Bowl.

Girls - if a guy you like asks you what you're doing on Super Bowl Sunday, it's okay to say you're not watching the game. But for godsakes, do not say "why, what's Sunday?"

It's a good thing the Fourth of July comes during the summertime. Any holiday where the country is encouraged to light explosives might be dangerous to celebrate while college is in session.

The coinciding of Mother's Day with finals is just poor timing. "Hey mom, guess what I got you! Bs!

Professors are sensitive to holidays of their culture, but don't cut you slack for your holidays. So if you get a druid professor, you can take off for the great fire festivals, but don't even try to explain Good Friday.

CHAPTER 10
THE END

I started writing the material for this book when I was a junior in college. Well, the first time I was a junior in college, since half way through that year I took a year off to work. Actually, I started writing the material for this book during the first week of my freshman year, but I only started writing it down a few years later. But I finished it two weeks after graduation, allowing myself to write from various perspectives as I experienced more of college life. And this is perhaps the weirdest perspective I've had – that brief period between college student and alum, where I haven't started work yet but I don't have anything to study for. Like a test on the rules governing dangling prepositions.

By the time you read this, I'll be a 9to5er, unless you're reading it with a million people. Then I can retire to a life of writing at 3PM while still in my boxers. So maybe I could be a college student forever.

My college experience was no more interesting than anyone else's, except for the experience of that squirrelly guy in the corner of my Calc class. And that's why this book was about *our* college experience. I tried to cover all of the universal crap that happens to eighteen to twenty-two-year-olds whose fake IDs say that they're twenty-one to twenty-five. And there's still a ton of things I haven't written about, but that's for the sequel. Oooh, I set that one up even better than Spiderman, and that whole movie was just a big commercial for the sequel.

I know I write a lot about drinking and skipping class, and other things that you're parents wouldn't like even though they've done them, too. Except if your dad is the squirrelly guy in the corner of my Calc class. Either way, my point is not to promote these things, rather to accept that they, like communal bathrooms, Instant Messenger, and mail rooms that steal and break stuff, are a part of college. The great thing about college is that regardless of if you want to study, party, do both, or do neither, there will be a place for you somewhere. Just make sure, wherever that place is, you look around and have a sense of humor about it all. Otherwise, college, and more so life, is no fun at all.

Now to paraphrase the immortal Ferris Bueller, it's over - go home. This is the end of college.

The Job Hunt

First semester, I said I was looking for work "in sports-writing." Over break, said, "in writing." By May, I said, "in America."

People told me I should go to grad school instead of working so I can be well-rounded. As if my four years of college didn't round me enough. I took two years of core classes before I could even start my major, and once I started, I still had to take four classes outside of my discipline. If I become anymore well-rounded, I can find a cushy job as a meatball.

Career fairs are supposed to help you decide what you want to do. Except the only companies that come to my school's career fair are firms like Goldman Sachs and Morgan Stanley. "Have you ever thought about an exciting career in finance? No? What about one in finance?"

Companies who fire veteran employees in order to hire cheaper recent college graduates are unscrupulous. They also don't return my calls.

I think "internship" is French for "we ain't payin you squat." Why French? Because to describe most internships, you'd have to pardon mine.

No matter how tempting, do *not* start sleeping with someone at work. If things go wrong with someone in one of your classes, you can sit on the other side of the room and ignore them by pretending to take notes. But at work, your boss decides who you're working with and where. And you can't tell them the truth. "I'm sorry sir, you can't put me on that project. Why? I banged her. Thanks for understanding."

Once I'm in a position to hire people for internships, I'm going to play favorites with my school. I had to work my butt off and kiss more ass than a submissive in a Times Square sex dungeon to get an internship my junior year. And then the only thing I ended up qualified to do afterwards was work as a submissive in a Times Square sex dungeon.

Some people advise you against taking the first job that comes your way just to pay off your billions in student loans. They say that you should scrimp and save in a piddling position in your industry so that you can eventually end up where you really want. Like debtor's prison.

Moving Out

At my school, you have plenty of time to move out after your last final. It's at least three hours.

Moving out is sad because it's the last time you'll see any of your floormates again. I'm not talking about seniors - I'm talking about freshmen who realize that they're only friends with these people because they happen to live down the hall.

Those little carts you get from your school to help move your stuff out of your dorm are a godsend. The carts are the perfect size to carry one or two of your possessions at once so it takes you only fourteen trips instead of twenty.

When seniors move out, they have a ton of extra stuff that they just give away for free. Bookshelves, TV carts, even alcohol. And though most freshmen don't own books or TVs, if you ever ask a freshman for free alcohol, you'd have a better chance of getting a college bookstore to give you full price for a used notebook.

You spend the last days of school alternating between packing and parent-proofing your room. You don't realize how many liquor bottles, cigarette cartons, and drunken pictures of yourself you own until you try to hide them all at once. You're going to say it so much, you may as well have "those are my roommate's" tattooed on your forehead.

Why do freshmen throw furniture out of windows? It's instinct - the same reason seniors turn the freshman in to their RA.

When you move in freshman year, you own two duffel bags of clothes, a computer, half a bottle of shampoo, maybe a guitar, probably a stereo, and some new notebooks. By the time you leave, you also have a TV, a mini fridge, an illegal halogen lamp, $800 worth of books no one would buy, some CDs you liked for a month two years ago, two dozen pint glasses you stole from the bar, two dozen spoons you stole from the dining hall, a futon, snap together shelves that look like hibachis, three dinner plates that don't match, and hundreds of pictures of you and your friends piss drunk. Just the right stuff to start your new life.

Graduation

A lot of people ask me what I'm going to do after graduation. I think I'll go to dinner with my parents, then drink a whole lot and pass out.

You have to write something in masking tape on your mortarboard—the space is too good to waste. I'm deciding between "thank you, Spark Notes," "for a good time call," and "brought to you by yahoo.com."

They tell us throwing our hats is dangerous. They're talking to people who spent the last four years drinking ourselves to sleep on the weekends, taking no-dos to study on the weekdays, subsisting solely pizza and Chinese food, and braving communal bathrooms regardless of whether or not we remembered to bring our shower shoes. If that didn't kill us, I don't think we have to worry about an out of control hat.

If you're not worried about getting into grad school, all you need is a B to get a job. So if you're through three years of school with A's and you find yourself not going to grad school, the only math you'll need to do is figure out exactly how many classes you can miss and still pass.

Graduation robes are so weird. Why do we only look educated after we dress up like giant colored snow angels?

I don't like the term "super senior." I prefer "redshirt academic."

High school juniors should know every question they'll will be asked for ten years. The first two,it's what college they'll attend. The next three, it's what their major is. The following year, it's what kind of job they're looking for. And for the remaining four, it's what college they went to, what they majored in, and what job they have.

Graduation is a huge step in a young adult's life. Hooking up with a college student goes from encouraged to sketchy in just three hours.

College is designed so you can do dumb things and look back later and say, "Hey, that was college." Go on, try it. "Sure, I ate four tons of Ramen noodles. Yeah, I hooked up with all my friends. Okay, I spent every week drinking myself unconscious. But hey - that was college."

CollegeHumor.com

laugh.

The Math of Dating

A Student Body Shots Special Feature

By Steve Hofstetter and Adam Schenk

These have been proven through years of experimental research.

I'm not all that good at math - in fact, an engineer and a math major helped me put this together. But what I do understand is that dating is screwy, and we could all use a little help understanding the rules. So here are a few of said rules, in no particular order.

1)   *The Constant Total Asset Theorem*
   $(x)*(y)=k$

Let x = beauty and y = intelligence of a particular subject, where k is a constant. Thus, as an individual's beauty increases, that same individual's intelligence decreases proportionately, and vice versa.

2)   *The Rule of Rarity*
   As k $\to$ oo, Ld $\to$ 0 and a $\to$ –(oo)

As the aforementioned constant k, defined as an individual's beauty multiplied by their intelligence, increases, the likelihood of discovery of this individual lessens towards zero, and this individual's availability approaches negative infinity.

3)   *The Theorem of Evening Odds*
   As $\dfrac{|(m\text{-}f)|}{|(f\text{+}m)|}$ $\to$ 1, Lmh $\to$ 0

Let m = males and f = females. As the ratio of men to women departs from equaling one in either direction, the likelihood of a male having a successful hookup decreases.

4)   *Corollary to the Theorem of Evening Odds*
   If (m >= 1) and (f >=1) and (Fd >=1), Lfh = 100%

Let fD represent the desire of one female. When there is at least one male and one female, and the female has a desire greater or equal to one, the likelihood of a girl hooking up is 100%.

5) *The Lady's Law*
   fD + mD = tDc + mD

Let mD represent the desire of one male. A female's desire plus a male's desire equals the total desire that counts plus a male's desire. After subtracting a male's desire from both sides, a female's desire equals the total desire that counts.

6) *The Rule of the DUFF*
   If h_i exsists, d_i exsists.
   X(h_i) + X(d_i) = 10

Let i represent any particular group of girls. Let H_i represent the hottie of the group. If H_i exists, there also exists a D_i, where D_i represents the Designated Ugly Fat Friend (DUFF). X(f) equals the score of a female's beauty on the standard 1-10 scale. Thus, the score of a hottie plus the score of her DUFF will always equal 10.

7) *The Wall Test Proof*
   If (b-w) > 0, (mD) > 0
   If w =< 30, as b-w → 12, mD increases
   If w > 30, mD = 0
   If w > 50, mD = -(oo)

Let b represent an individual's breast size and w represent an individual's waist size. If breast size minus waist size is greater than zero, the desire of a particular male is greater than zero. If waist size is less than or equal to thirty, as breast size minus waist size approaches twelve, the desire of a male increases. If waist size is greater than thirty, the desire of a male equals zero. If waste size is greater than fifty, well, you do the math.

8) *The John Nash Theory of Dating:* Prisoner's Dilemma

3/ 3	5 / 0
0 / 5	1 / 1

When faced with a one-time choice, it is usually most beneficial to do what is best for you. However, when faced with a situation where you must choose several times, it is usually most beneficial to do what is best for the collective.

STEVE HOFSTETTER'S
i don't want a real job
2002-2003 TOUR

Columbia U.	NY	09.12.02	UniversityBookstore
Meredith College	NC	09.21.02	MEA
Lehigh U.	PA	11.06.02	AMA
Embry Riddle U.	FL	01.20.03	Sigma Pi
Kettering U.	MI	02.18.03	Greek Council
Indiana U.	IN	03.01.03	Zeta Beta Tau
Fresno State U.	CA	03.10.03	Phi Gamma Delta
U. Rochester	NY	03.20.03	Kappa Delta
Drexel U.	PA	04.02.03	Pi Kappa Alpha
Temple U.	PA	04.03.03	IFC
Kenyon College	OH	04.10.03	Sophomore Class
Elmhurst College	IL	04.11.03	Union Board
College of NJ	NJ	04.24.03	Greek Council
Washburn U.	KS	04.25.03	Greek Council
Rutgers-Newark	NJ	04.27.03	Tau Kappa Epsilon

COMING TO A CAMPUS NEAR YOU.

booking@observationalhumor.com

Don't Believe the Hype

A Student Body Shots Special Feature
Originally Written for the Columbia Daily Spectator

I am a college student. This is what the world thinks of me.

I stay up late. I wake up later. I still need to sleep in class—when I go to class.

I yell things at the top of my lungs, like "party!" or "spring break!" or "college!" I have mp3 copies of every Dave Matthews CD ever released, and I didn't pay for any of them. My room is covered in posters – especially that one of John Belushi in a shirt that says "College" and the guy with the windy cheeks from that Maxell ad. I live in a frat house.

Sometimes I play drinking games with my friends. Sometimes I play drinking games with myself. I always drink five or more beers in one sitting.

I eat pizza for breakfast (when I have breakfast), Ramen for lunch, and I'm on the meal plan for dinner. I constantly complain about the meal plan, but I take seconds anyway. Cargo pants are the perfect size for bagels.

Classes bore me, and I take the easiest ones possible. I don't study until a few hours before my exam, after I'm up all night on Ritalin. I'm dumb unless I'm double majoring in the hard sciences. I am not double majoring in the hard sciences.

I have a bong in my room. My RA allows it because she doesn't know what a bong looks like, and I tell her it's a hookah. I do not know what a hookah looks like.

I like sex. I like sex a lot. It's all I think about, and every time I leave my dorm room, it's with the express purpose of having sex. Sometimes, I don't have to leave my room because people come to have sex with me—usually while my roommate is trying to study.

I desperately want a job, but I am too irresponsible to do anything except make copies. Sometimes I screw those up too. But no one else will make copies all summer for eight dollars an hour because no one else is as poor as I am. Companies like hiring people as poor as I am.

When I run out of Dave Matthews MP3s, I listen to Phish covering Dave Matthews. When I can't do that, I listen to a few guys from the next dorm who cover Phish covering Dave Matthews. One day, I hope to get a band together so that we can cover them.

I use the Cliffs Notes to write my papers, but I'm too lazy to read them all the way through. I'd rather do research online than in a library.

I judge how cool I am by how seldom I go to the library. I think I'm pretty cool.

I use Instant Messenger twenty-three and a half hours a day. I have three different away messages for every activity I'm involved in and I have two screen names so I can check who is on-line. I was thrilled when AOL upped the limit on buddy lists, so I could add more people that my roommate stalks. I IM my roommate.

I use words like "sketchy" and "tool" and expect my parents to know what I mean. When I go home over break, I argue about sleeping in the same room with whoever I'm dating. My mother does not do my laundry fast enough. My father found the condoms in my night table, but is trying to be cool about it.

I am on my third cell phone. I lost one in a bar and smashed the other one while I was just as smashed. I have twelve dozen numbers stored in my phone but I don't know who half of them belong to. It takes me an hour to get ready—unless it's for class. I can do that in thirty seconds.

Free food will get me to go anywhere. I'm not active in any clubs but I'm on thirty-seven different mailing lists. I love all of my school's teams, even though I can't name anyone on them. Except for that guy on my freshman floor. You know, what's-his-name.

I am terrified of graduation because I don't have a job lined up. Maybe I'll go backpacking in Europe. Maybe I'll go to law school even though I have no intention of becoming a lawyer. It doesn't matter – my parents will pay for it.

Eventually I'll find a job. Then I'll become a young professional. I'll get a studio apartment for a year or two until I earn enough to move into a one-bedroom. All the furniture I own will still be made of particleboard. I'll try to go out at night, but I'll be too tired after work. So I'll turn on the TV and see news stories about these damn college kids yelling "party!" and ruining the music industry and doing everything they can to disrupt the lives of everyone who is not in college anymore. And hopefully, I'll know better than to believe it.

Just when you thought it was safe to go back to college...

Student Body Shots: Another Round
more sarcasm on the best 4-6 years of your life
By Steve Hofstetter
with Matt Boor and Court Sullivan
foreword by Spanky

08.03